Three Touches

Three Touches

Jacob Hilden Winslow

RESOURCE *Publications* • Eugene, Oregon

THREE TOUCHES

Resource Publications
An Imprint of Wipf and Stock Publishers
199 W. 8th Ave., Suite 3
Eugene, OR 97401

www.wipfandstock.com

PAPERBACK ISBN: 979-8-3852-7342-3
HARDCOVER ISBN: 979-8-3852-7343-0
EBOOK ISBN: 979-8-3852-7344-7

VERSION NUMBER 03/16/26

What I dare ask of them all—what I have the right to expect of their sense of justice—is that they not hurry to judge from the outside what can be judged only from within and concerns only inner truth. . . . Only the reflective conscience of any good-faith reader, curious to know himself, can answer the call my book makes to him.

—Maine de Biran
Nouveaux essais d'anthropologie

Contents

Preface

The first touch, *Phaedrus 2.0*, raises the question, *What is* This? and partially tears it from the context of philosophy. The second touch, *Soft Words and Dry Thoughts*, adresses the question from within and without philosophy, while the third touch, *When Leaving the Palace*, sings the praise of surrendering to This.

The sections *In the Land of Projects, Mine,* and *Home at Last* in *Soft Words and Dry Thoughts* are based on the book *Travels in Me,* which I published under the names Axel Lidenbrock & Hother Holgersen. Some of the poems in *When Leaving the Palace* have been published in various little magazines.

Jacob Hilden Winslow

Phaedrus 2.0

Prefatory Note

The action takes place around 410 BCE, just outside Athens' Thriasian Gate. It was here that Phaedrus and Socrates met one summer's day to discuss—for the first time in recorded history—the role of language in the love of wisdom. And it was here, in the crown of the oak above their resting place, that the *Dead Philosophers' Club* held its centennial assembly. The following pages recount the conversation between Phaedrus and Socrates, and what came of it when a few others decided to take part.

Dramatis Personae

PHAEDRUS (ca. 444–393 BCE), a citizen of Athens, recently returned from ten years of exile for mocking the goddess Demeter.

SOCRATES (ca. 470–399 BCE), his friend and teacher, who, ten years after this conversation with Phaedrus, allowed himself to be condemned to death because he insisted on being who he was—a lover of wisdom.

PLATO, i.e., **YOUNG PLATO** and **OLD PLATO** (427–348 BCE): a philosopher and Socrates' principal biographer, author of a series of dialogues including the *Phaedrus*.

IMMANUEL KANT (1724–1804), a German philosopher, popularizer of the concept *a priori*.

JOHN NIEMEYER FINDLAY (1903–1987), a hardworking Hegel-inspired South African philosopher.

JULES AYER (1910–1989), an English philosopher who imported logical positivism from Austria to England.

KARL POPPER (1902–1994), an Austrian-English philosopher of science, godfather of critical rationalism.

OSHO, a.k.a. **RAJNEESH** (1931–1990), an Indian mystic who combined broad familiarity with Western philosophy with a mix of Hinduism, Sufism, and Buddhism.

EMMANUEL LEVINAS (1906–1995), a Lithuanian-French philosopher, widely recognized (and occasionally blamed) for making "the Other" everyone's problem.

SIMONE WEIL (1909–1943), a French philosopher who, like Socrates, allowed her convictions to lead her to death.

JACQUES DERRIDA, a.k.a. **JACKIE** (1930–2004), a French philosopher, parent of concepts like deconstruction, *différance*, and *la trace*.

SIGMUND FREUD (1856–1939) and **KARL MARX** (1818–1883), each a defining icon of modernity's self-understanding.

Act One

Outside the city walls of Athens, near the Thriasian Gate. PHAEDRUS is walking, grey-skinned with fatigue after a morning spent at Epikrates' house, where the assembled guests had been discussing Lysias' latest speech on love.

PHAEDRUS: Phew, that was a tough morning! Maybe a short walk outside the city walls, where birdsong replaces the boom of men's voices, can clear my head. . . Wait, who is that lying under the oak tree? He's calling out to me. *(PHAEDRUS approaches the man.)*

SOCRATES: Hello, Phaedrus. Where have you been, and where are you going? And what's happening in between those two points, i.e., what are you thinking of?

PHAEDRUS: I've been at Epikrates' house, listening to Lysias' speech on love.

SOCRATES: Love! A delightful topic. So why do you look so gloomy?

PHAEDRUS: Ah, Socrates . . . As you know, during my exile I sailed the Aegean, seeking out the wisdom of the sages. I listened to Thales' followers, who claimed everything is water, and to Heraclitus' students, who claimed it is fire, and to many others. And now I'm back in Athens, not one bit wiser.

SOCRATES: Hmm. I doubt that's entirely true. Surely you've picked up something from the sages' tables. But for now, you've come straight from Epikrates' table and Lysias' speech. What did you take from it?

PHAEDRUS: That's probably why I'm downcast. Because as I listened to all those words about what love is, it hit me: Lysias was turning love into something else, he was turning it into *words*. And the same goes for all the wise men I listened to in Miletus and Ephesus and other places. They turned *what is*—the thing I'm seeking—into *words*. And by doing so, they betrayed it. What do you think, Socrates?

SOCRATES: Honestly? I have no idea. But here comes my good friend and your wise cousin, Plato. Let's ask him. He's always good for a word or five. *(PLATO, a youth of nearly twenty, walks toward them.)*

PHAEDRUS: Hey, cousin. Did you hear what I just told Socrates?

PLATO: I caught the end of it. May I try rephrasing your thought in my own words?

PHAEDRUS: Please! anything that brings more clarity!

PLATO: Right. So you're saying:

Firstly, when we ask, "What is that which is?", we imply that what exists might be something other than how it appears, that is, we presuppose a deeper reality behind the appearances.

And, *secondly*, when we seek the answer to that question in language we turn *what is* into *a description*, which betrays reality itself.

Is that a fair rendering of your point, cousin?

PHAEDRUS: Yes, I think so. The way you've broken it down certainly sounds much more polished than what I said.

PLATO: All right then. In the first part of your reasoning, you suggest the question points toward something beneath the surface, something more *real* than what appears. What could that be? Hmm . . . Good question. We're both familiar with Thales' idea of everything as water, and Heraclitus' idea of everything as fire, and many others. But they all make the same mistake: they equate the fundamental with something drawn from superficial reality. I mean, water is water and fire is fire, right? That deeper reality your question points to must be something essentially different from what our senses show us . . .

PHAEDRUS: But cousin, I don't think you quite understand my problem . . . *(A loud crack is heard from the oak tree above, and OLD PLATO drops down from the branches.)*

OLD PLATO: Socrates! You can't be serious—letting that clueless kid represent my views? I never did anything like that to you!

SOCRATES, PHAEDRUS and YOUNG PLATO *(in a startled chorus)*: Who are you???

OLD PLATO: I'm Plato, Socrates' main biographer, author of the *Phaedrus*, the *Republic*, the *Symposium*, and a few other modest contributions where I give crystal-clear answers to Phaedrus' question about what truly is. . . . Why are you all staring? Oh, right, sorry. You're not supposed to be able to see me. One of life's little mysteries. The thing is, the *Dead Philosophers' Club* is holding its general assembly in this very oak. We meet once every century at a site of philosophical significance, like this tree, under which Socrates once taught Phaedrus about the love of wisdom.

SOCRATES: Must've been in another cosmos . . . ?

OLD PLATO: Nonsense, Socrates. The idea of parallel universes wasn't even remotely precise enough back when you and Phaedrus met for you to claim that. Let's get back to Phaedrus' question.

YOUNG PLATO: I'm going home to nurse my headache. I don't think I'm ready to hear what's coming . . .

OLD PLATO: Good idea, my young friend. You'll get there when both you and time have matured enough. (*Exit YOUNG PLATO.*) Now, Phaedrus, listen closely. The question that drove you to sail the Aegean in search of answers—a question that, by the way, does you credit—was: *What is that which is?* That is the first step toward recognizing true reality.

Let me illustrate with an image from my dialogue, *The Republic*:

Imagine an underground cave, where people have lived all their lives, chained so they can only see the wall in front of them. Behind them burns a fire, and between the fire and the prisoners move objects casting shadows on the wall. These shadows are all they can see, and they take them for reality.

Now imagine one prisoner's chains fall off. At first he just shifts around, maybe stands up to stretch. But slowly he turns toward the fire behind him. He sees, for the first time, the objects and people whose shadows he had mistaken for reality. It hurts to look, but little by little he adjusts. Then he's drawn further, out into the daylight beyond the cave. First he's blinded, but gradually the world opens up: the sky, the land, the sun itself.

And then he understands: all he once thought real was only a pale reflection of something richer, more real. The shadows were mere imitations of eternal Forms, which now stand revealed before him.

So, Phaedrus, when someone asks, *What is that which is?* that is a beginning. A step away from shadows, toward what truly is: the Forms.

PHAEDRUS: But cousin, I don't think you quite got what I was trying to say. Because . . . *(A voice from the tree canopy interrupts, and IMMANUEL KANT drops down.)*

KANT: Apologies, gentlemen. I was visiting the little house after Nietzsche, and the stench was so bad I had to open a window. And then I couldn't help but overhear your fascinating discussion. May I join? I'm Kant, professor of logic and metaphysics at the University of Königsberg.

SOCRATES: Certainly, good sir. But where is Königsberg? And what's a professor?

KANT: Ah, dear Socrates, of course you don't know me, though you will get to know me in about ten years' time. But rest assured, I know *you*. Königsberg lies so far from Athens that even your prodigious imagination couldn't conceive it, so I won't try to explain. Professors are civil servants in the modern state, appointed by a prince or other authority to transmit wisdom to the more privileged of its subjects.

SOCRATES: Never mind Königsberg. I've no wish to leave Athens anyway. But I still don't quite follow the thing about professors. In my time—*our* time (*gestures at Phaedrus*)—the love of wisdom is cultivated by free citizens, beholden to no one, in the marketplace. There are scoundrels who take money to teach those same citizens how to confuse others like our friend Phaedrus here. But people who are *paid* to spread the love of wisdom to others' subjects? That I've never heard of . . .

KANT: I understand, Socrates. But let's return to our friend Phaedrus' reasoning and the venerable Plato's comments.

PLATO: Very well, I'll continue . . .

KANT (*interrupting*): My apologies, noble Plato! But before you proceed, may I ask three brief questions about your vivid allegory?

PLATO (*grumbling*): Oh, fine. I remember what I was going to say—*I* don't need a script.

KANT: My questions all concern the prisoner's process of recognition: How does it begin? When is it complete? And why doesn't he stop along the way?

You said, Plato, that once the man's eyes adjust to the fire, he begins to *suspect* that the objects are more real than the shadows. But what prompts that suspicion? Why doesn't he simply panic and run back to what he knows?

Next: what drives him onward toward the cave's mouth? How does he know the light above won't reveal something terrifying, some threat rather than a truth?

And finally: when he stands in the sunlight, seeing the world in all its splendor, how can he know *this* is the real reality? How can he be sure that somewhere else, say atop a mountain or deep in a valley, he won't find a third source of light, revealing something even *more* real?

PLATO: Kant, it's an *allegory*. Try walking with it, instead of trying to stop it before you've even had the benefit of the journey.

KANT (*somewhat sheepish*): Yes, of course. My apologies for the untimely interruption. I suppose I'm too accustomed to dealing with dim-witted sons of Prussian junkers, whose imaginations couldn't fill a single acorn of this oak. Please, Plato, continue with your exposition.

PLATO: Thank you. As I was saying: the allegory shows how what most people mistake for reality—the shadows on a flat wall—relates to what *truly* is: the unchanging, eternal Forms. When someone asks, "What is that which is?", I believe they begin a search that will eventually lead beyond the realm of shadows, toward a stable reality, toward *what is*, in contrast to what merely *becomes*.

PHAEDRUS: The Forms, with a capital F, I hear. And how do they differ from the forms we enjoy when a pretty young woman passes by in the marketplace?

PLATO: Ah, cousin. That's not entirely the wrong image. But it's not *her* I'm speaking of.

Imagine a chair in an old home. The chair you see isn't perfect. It might be a little loose at the joints, the paint worn off in places, the seat stained by wine or worse. Yet behind all that, we glimpse a faint shadow of what a *true* chair should be.

Now take a circle. When you draw one in the sand, it will never be exact, only a copy of the perfect, unchanging circle that exists in the world of ideas. The same goes for beauty and justice. When we perceive something beautiful, we don't just see color and shape, we glimpse a reflection of eternal Beauty, which never changes.

That's why the world of Forms matters: it gives us a fixed measure of truth and goodness. Our senses deceive us. But reason can lead us closer to what is.

The highest of all the Forms is the Good. As the sun gives light and life, the Good illuminates our minds and makes knowledge possible. It is the source of the Forms, and by striving toward the Good, we can live in harmony with true reality.

So when Thales says, "All is water," and Heraclitus says, "All is fire," I respond: No. What we see are pale imitations of the eternal Forms, which alone are truly real.

PHAEDRUS: Beautifully said, cousin. But it still doesn't quite speak to the problem I'm trying to understand. What troubled me about Lysias' speech this morning was not just what he said about love, it was the fact that, *by speaking*, he turned love into something *other than* love. He made it into words.

And the same was true of Thales, Heraclitus, and all the others I listened to in my exile. They turned *what is*—the thing I seek—into *words*. And in doing so, they betrayed it. I think you're doing it too—wait, what's that? *(A wailing is heard, distant at first, then nearer. It comes from a slave passing by the oak, accompanied by his master and the master's two sons. The master walks ahead, holding the hand of the youngest. The slave moans beneath rhythmic blows from the elder son, who seems more focused on his father and younger brother than on the beating he is giving to the slave.)*

PLATO: Yes . . . what might be going on there? . . . In any case, I concede your point: language, tied to the ever-changing sensory world, often fails to grasp the unchanging Forms. It may seem, at times, to betray the truth.

But the solution is not silence. It is *more* speech! Not just any speech, but precise questions and responses in a dialectical process. Through clarification of concepts and testing for contradiction, thought can be led from confused opinions to clear insight into the Forms.

Even though language is often abused—by rhetoricians like Lysias or in everyday chatter—I see dialectical dialogue as a ladder for the soul: a tool for lifting us from the visible toward the intelligible. This world of Forms is not a closed realm. It is accessible to all, through recollection from previous lives: what we call *anamnēsis*. That's why I don't believe language necessarily betrays. It can become our path to truth.

Allow me to illustrate with a conversation between Socrates and a slave boy, which I recorded in the *Meno*. And since we have Socrates himself here today, he can vouch for my account.

SOCRATES: If you say so. *(He clearly has no memory of the* Meno.*)*

PLATO: In *Meno*, the conversation reaches what's called *Meno's paradox*: how can we learn anything if we know nothing? Where do we search—and how can we recognize what we're looking for?

Socrates responds with the idea of *anamnēsis*: that the soul already knows, but has forgotten. He offers to prove this by asking questions of a slave boy—one chosen by Meno himself. Through questioning, Socrates guides the boy to consider how to double the area of a square. The boy first answers incorrectly that the sides must be twice as long. But with further guidance, he realizes the sides must equal the diagonal of the original square.

Meno must admit that Socrates has done nothing but ask questions. Socrates concludes: the boy already held the knowledge within him. He just needed help remembering it.

KANT: My dear Plato, a model rendering of one of philosophy's great classics.

SOCRATES *(aside, to Phaedrus)*: "One of philosophy's great classics"? What *is* this man talking about?

KANT *(as if he hadn't heard)*: Allow me to offer an alternative reading of the dialogue between Socrates and the slave boy, one that doesn't rely on an immortal soul or memories from past lives.

What we see here is not recollection, but an expression of the *a priori* structures on which all cognition depends, those conditions the mind already possesses before experience begins. The boy doesn't rediscover forgotten knowledge. He constructs new insight through his innate capacity to understand spatial relations.

Socrates does guide him with questions, yes. But he also draws figures in the sand. The crucial point is that the boy grasps the relation between sides and area through spatial *intuition*. Geometric knowledge is an example of *synthetic a priori* knowledge: it doesn't come from experience alone, but from cognitive tools we already have.

Thus, the conversation is proof not of memory, but of reason's power to construct knowledge actively.

PLATO: But that's just—as you rightly say—a different *story* than mine. And frankly, it's a story that would convince a man of your time more than one of mine. From where do you get your "a priori structures," these "necessary forms of the mind" and "innate cognitive faculties"? Can you explain that in a way a man of my time might understand?

KANT: I'll try. Imagine all knowledge coming from looking at the world through a pair of lenses we're born with. These lenses—what we call *a priori* conditions—aren't something we learn from experience; they're the very tools that *make* experience possible. Without them, the colorful images we receive from our senses would be chaotic and meaningless.

PLATO: But you still haven't told me where these lenses or structures come from.

KANT: You've hit the crucial point. These *a priori* conditions are part of human nature itself; they're the very foundation of how we perceive and structure the world. We can't ask "where" they come from in an empirical sense—they're not *given by* nature; they're what *make nature intelligible* to us. They are the inborn features of our reason that allow us to synthesize sensory input into knowledge.

PLATO: So when I say "immortal soul," you say "innate cognitive structures" or "lenses." Is that about right?

KANT: Yes, you could put it that way—crudely, but aptly.

PLATO: What a bleak story. Where is Helen's beauty, Hector's courage in all this? And what about the courage we know our friend Socrates will show in ten years, when he'll have the chance to save his life by recanting, and doesn't? Where are beauty, goodness, and justice? Where is the highest Good?

KANT: Dear Plato, I understand your concern, and I appreciate your examples. Here, we're not so far apart.

Let me clarify: What I call phenomena is the world as we experience it, structured by our senses and intellect: space, time, and concepts. That's the reality we can know.

But just as you speak of the Forms, we must assume something behind the phenomena: what I call the *noumena*. Our knowledge needs a backdrop, a reality independent of our perception, which our senses and concepts can shape into something meaningful. Without that assumption, everything would appear random and unintelligible.

We can't know the noumena directly, but assuming their existence lets us explain why the world appears ordered, and why concepts like beauty, goodness, and justice can have universal value.

So, my dear friend we're actually quite close in spirit . . . And isn't it time we were on a first-name basis?

PLATO: Gladly, Immanuel . . .

SOCRATES (*to Phaedrus*): I think what we're hearing here is the beginning of something I'm not entirely sure I want to hear the rest of . . .

PLATO (*ignoring Socrates*): But I still think you make my world very small, Immanuel—when you deny me access to the Good through dialectic. It becomes a world so small, it could fit inside a schoolboy's pencil case. From being something we can strive toward, you reduce the Good to something we must assume, just to make sense of our experience. It's a very small world, Immanuel.

KANT: Ah . . . yes, perhaps you're right, dear friend. But Königsberg *was* a very small town in my time. Still, let me point out two small rays of hope for your longing for a larger world: the *categorical imperative* and the *sublime.*

The categorical imperative is the principle that says we should only act according to that maxim which we can at the same time will to become universal law. It's an attempt to ground morality in reason itself, in what applies to all, regardless of desire, culture, or circumstance. Duty, then, becomes not an external demand, but an expression of our rational nature. When we act out of duty, we act as free beings.

PLATO: But it's still all inside the pencil case, though now in a very well-behaved schoolboy's pencil case. What about the thing you call the sublime?

KANT: The sublime is that before which all else seems small. When you come from a town as tiny as Königsberg—one-tenth the size of your Athens—it's easy to be impressed: the weight of the Earth, the distance to the Moon, the number of hairs on the cats in Egypt.

But even greater are the numbers the imagination can conceive: 10 to the 100th, 2.7 to the 100,000,000th. That's dizzying. But still something the mind can grasp. Now imagine a series where each number is the square of the previous one. It goes on and on . . . but where does it end? The imagination can't contain it.

This is where reason steps in. It *thinks* the infinite and completes the sequence with three dots. We shiver at our limitation, and rejoice in reason's power to exceed it.

And isn't that, Plato, what your ideas of beauty, justice, and the Good point to? That reason reaches beyond the bounds of experience? *(A thump is heard, and a voice calls out.)*

FINDLAY: Pardon me, I dropped my satchel. Would someone be kind enough to hand it up to me?

KANT: Findlay! Still grading papers? Is the general assembly that boring?

FINDLAY: Yawn—yes! We're stuck reviewing the proposed bylaws, and Kripke and Putnam are at it again, arguing about how long one has to be tenured to qualify for club membership. And I promised my students they'd get these essays back on Monday.

KANT: But dear Findlay, you're not only retired. You're dead! Surely no students are still waiting for feedback?

FINDLAY: Well, you never know when they might show up. Or down, as may be more accurate. And I didn't finish grading this set before I passed on.

But what are *you* two doing down there on Earth? We only rented the canopy for our general assembly.

KANT: We came down because young Phaedrus here asked an interesting question—one I've now forgotten, to be honest—and then Plato and I got into a bit of a scuffle over whether humans can access what I call noumena and he calls the Forms. Just before you dropped your satchel, he accused me of making the world so small it could fit inside a schoolboy's pencil case. Or perhaps, he said, inside the human being.

FINDLAY *(climbing down the trunk)*: You know what, Kant? I think Plato's right. You never really grasped Hegel's spirit. Let me try to explain where you went wrong in Königsberg, and how we might make the world a little bigger again.

Let me begin with a simple question: how do you feel when you wake up in the morning, compared to when you were fifteen?

PLATO and KANT (*in unison*): Miserable. Exhausted. Stiff everywhere except where stiffness would be interesting.

FINDLAY: Exactly. Everything feels unsatisfying. But that's not the whole truth. Because in reality, everything is exactly as it should be. When we put our feet on the floor, we don't step into a void, or a lion's mouth. The moon does not crash into our heads, gravity keeps it where it should be. Everything holds together, as long as we live. Our senses fit the world, and the world fits us. That's worth remembering, especially for philosophers.

And yet it *feels* all wrong. We long for another kind of life, one we neither fully know nor can describe. Christians, communists, and the rest of us try to find it in ideas, visions, or Netflix series (yes, we have those down here too). But the satisfying life never quite arrives—so we go to the next episode, the next imaginary world.

Kant, your followers called this a "metaphysical longing", and compared it to Plato's. But Plato was right: your longing fits in a pencil case. Your merit was to show how our ideas are shaped by that case. But you lost sight of what lies beyond it.

The task after you, then, became to *open* the case toward the world—to reunite ideas and reality. To overcome the opposition between "everything functions" and "nothing feels right." That's what Hegel tried to do.

KANT: But Findlay, your examples still stay inside the stuffy pencil case! They're psychological observations: the world is perfect but feels wrong to us. That might inspire doctrines of salvation, like Buddhism or Christianity. But it's not enough to ground a philosophy.

FINDLAY: You're absolutely right, Kant. The tension between what is and how we experience it is only interesting because it suggests that what is could be otherwise. But if we truly want to understand Phaedrus' sense of betrayal by the philosophers we have to go back to his original question: *What is that which is?* And that, in turn, requires us to clarify some things about words, concepts, logic, and argument—in short, about what Plato called dialectic.

Do you have time for that?

SOCRATES and **PHAEDRUS** (*in chorus*): Yes!

FINDLAY: Wonderful! I'm glad.

In Plato's dialectic, the central tool was the question: *What do you mean by that?* Through clarifying concepts, Socrates and his interlocutor would try to reach the clarity characteristic of the eternal Forms. This required consistent use of words and avoiding contradiction.

Plato's method is excellent for producing clarity, but not always for developing thoughts that go beyond what language already contains. For that, concepts must be allowed to move—to shift meaning along the way. That is one of the insights we owe to Hegel. Let me give you an image:

A country is suddenly under threat. A young man—a student, pacifist by inclination, raised alone by his mother—volunteers for the army. The threat touches him deeply, and his decision brings him peace. But when he tries to explain his motives—to his mother, to a friend, to a teacher—he gives different answers: to his mother, he speaks of her values; to the teacher, of constitutional principles; to the friend, of his manliness. None of the explanations fully capture his motives. But in the act itself, he knows there is something he wants to protect. Maybe, later, he'll find the right words. Maybe not. But he knows that there is something he wants to protect.

An outsider would only see that he uses different language depending on who he's speaking to, and perhaps frown at it. But in philosophy we must seek this kind of flexibility and free ourselves from excessive logic-chopping. Thought must be allowed to evolve before the concepts are fully formed.

PLATO: So do the laws of logic no longer matter to you?

FINDLAY: On the contrary. It's *precisely* the violations of logic's rules that show us the way forward by revealing tensions and cracks in our understanding. But formal logic is syntactic: it treats words as fixed and static. A deeper logic must be semantic. It must allow concepts to evolve, contain contradictions, and relate to one another. *(The branches above part, releasing a thick cloud of French tobacco smoke. A goddess-like female face emerges from the haze, and a voice is heard.)*

SIMONE WEIL: Findlay, Plato, Kant—what are you all doing out there? It's time to vote. Get back up here! *(The three philosophers climb back into the oak canopy, leaving SOCRATES and PHAEDRUS alone.)*

SOCRATES: Well, Phaedrus, did your conversation with those philosophers bring you any clarity?

PHAEDRUS: No, Socrates, it didn't. I told you what disturbed me during Lysias' speech at Epikrates' house—that he turned love into something else by *speaking* of it; he made it into *words*. And that it was the same thing I'd experienced among the philosophers in Miletus and Ephesus during my exile. That by *talking* about what is, they *made it into something else*—and thus betrayed it.

Did Plato and Kant do the same? I don't think they truly understood me. Instead of entering into my problem—that words do something to what is, something that disturbs me—they eagerly pounced on my original question, the one I set out from Athens with: *What is that which is?* And there, they both agreed: to talk about what is as something entirely other, Plato's Forms, Kant's noumena.

Why is it that two such clever men are so bad at hearing what others say? And why are they so obsessed with proving that what is . . . isn't quite what is?

SOCRATES: You're asking more than I know. What about Findlay?

PHAEDRUS: Findlay's point about the need to keep concepts open and fluid in dialogue was interesting.

But again, like Kant and Plato he simply took for granted that philosophical dialogue is good, something worth pursuing. He, too, didn't really address my unease—that perhaps this kind of conversation *betrays* what is . . .

End of Act One

Act Two

A typical academic conference room. No windows. Bare walls. A constant hum from the air conditioning. Wall-to-wall carpet with a faint scent of industrial cleaner. PLATO, KANT, AYER, and POPPER are alone in the room.

AYER *(to Plato and Kant)*: Honestly, this is beyond the pale. You two trying to influence Phaedrus and Socrates before one of the most pivotal philosophical conversations in history? And then inviting Findlay—that Hegelian foghorn—to chime in as well? Can you not see the catastrophic consequences this might have for the history of philosophy? Not to mention that it's just plain unsporting, it isn't cricket—or rugby.

The conversation between Sokrates and Phaedrus may be the first real methodological debate in the history of science. About the proper use of language. And you let Findlay deliver his twisted gospel of conceptual slippage before the actual conversation has even begun—before Socrates has had the chance to drill his pupil in the rules of proper dialogue.

KANT: Well, I mean, it wasn't really our fault that Kripke and Putnam bored Findlay so much he left the general assembly.

AYER: Right, what's done is done, and perhaps the damage isn't too great. But you need to get hold of those two down there and bring them up here, so we can make sure they're on the right track before we leave them to each other again. Plato, call them up here, will you? You're the one who knows them best. *(Exit PLATO)*.

KANT *(meekly, to Popper, like a schoolboy in trouble)*: He said we invited Findlay. We didn't, though . . .

AYER: I can hear you, you know.

(The door opens. PLATO enters with SOCRATES and PHAEDRUS.)

SOCRATES *(looking around)*: So this is what Hades looks like. . .

AYER: Welcome, Phaedrus, Socrates. I'm Jules Ayer, former Wykeham Professor of Logic at Oxford. And this is Karl Popper, Professor of Logic and Scientific Method at the London School of Economics. We were both knighted by Queen Elizabeth II—so we're not just *anyone*.

SOCRATES *(murmurs something inaudible.)*

AYER *(ignoring him)*: Phaedrus, you told Socrates that your experience with philosophers across the Aegean was that they betrayed *what is*—by turning it into *words*. And I agree with you, at least at first glance. But here's the thing: the reason words could betray you, Phaedrus, is because *you* let yourself be seduced—by your own question: *What is that which is?* Shall I explain?

PHAEDRUS: Yes, please. If there's even a chance of gaining more clarity, I'll listen to anyone, anywhere—even here, in this gloomy tomb of a room. Do people really live like this? Is it only for noblemen? What did you do to deserve such a dreadful fate?

AYER: Of course people live here. Some of modern humanity's greatest intellectual triumphs are celebrated in rooms just like this. And no, it's not only for nobles. This place is rather like your agora, where everyone can come—provided they're not slaves or women or lack a certified PhD—and discuss ideas in search of wisdom, fame, and tenure. *(Socrates and Phaedrus exchange a look.)*

But let's get back to it: To understand why your question misled you, we need to take a closer look at language. There are two kinds of sentences: *attributive* ones, like "Socrates blushes," where something is said about a subject and *existential* ones, like "Socrates is," where we just assert that the subject exists.

SOCRATES: I honestly can't remember the last time I blushed. . .

AYER: These two sentence types look similar. And many philosophers have been fooled into thinking they mean the same thing. Especially when we use pronouns like "it"—as in "It is"—we're tempted to think there's some hidden subject we can meaningfully discuss. But as Kant rightly showed, existence isn't a property. Saying "Socrates is" adds nothing if we already know he blushes, speaks, and lives in Athens.

So when you ask, *What is that which is?* Phaedrus, you're asking a question that looks meaningful but doesn't actually point to anything we can meaningfully talk about. It lures you in.

PHAEDRUS: But what about people who claim that that which is is water? Or fire? Or my cousin Plato, who says that what truly is is the Forms?

AYER: Also seduced by language, Phaedrus. I'm sorry to say it, but you wasted ten years at sea . . . Maybe this will help: If I say, *The moon is made of green cheese,* what would you say?

PHAEDRUS: That's nonsense.

AYER: Yes. But *why*?

PHAEDRUS: Hmm . . . it just *is*?

AYER: No, Phaedrus—it's nonsense because you can't meaningfully check whether it's true. And that's the point: for a sentence to be meaningful, we must be able to say what would make it true or false. That's the verification principle.

Take Thales' claim, *Everything is actually water*. With a suitably flexible definition of "water," we can make the claim fit everything and thus contradict nothing. Which means, in effect, that it says nothing at all. It's like saying, *All men are men.*

PHAEDRUS: OK . . . but I still don't understand why my question makes no sense. It made perfect sense to *me* in all those years I sailed the Aegean.

AYER: Sure—but that's another kind of sense. *Emotional* sense.

Maybe your question helped you cope with exile, gave shape to your days.

If it's still with you now, after your return to Athens, maybe it's giving your life direction—just like Demeter's worshippers find hope in their rituals, which you mocked. But that doesn't mean you can expect a meaningful *answer* to your question. Because in truth, the only things that are are the things we can speak of meaningfully.

POPPER: But Ayer—what about your own verification principle? Is that meaningful? Or is it just another belief that gives your life structure—and lands you a professorship at Oxford?

PHAEDRUS: What do *you* mean, Popper?

POPPER: I mean: your question was a good one, Phaedrus. Not because it could be answered directly, but because it forced us to try. Philosophy began because someone said something wrong. Thales and Heraclitus cast their nets wide. Their claims may have been false, but they were the beginning. The same goes for you.

Instead of condemning their words as betrayal, you could have tried to weave them together: water as enduring, fire as change. Maybe the fusion of those ideas would have led you further. But instead, you stopped because their words didn't match your feeling.

PHAEDRUS: That might be true. And I get your point: you believe we must go on speaking. More speech, not silence, is needed to approach truth.

POPPER: Exactly! Because truth, Phaedrus, isn't a destination, it's a process. And words, even the clumsy ones, are our tools. Not traitors, but companions.

PLATO: You're still children, both of you. Language and the senses cast shadows—not truth. It takes more than net-casting to approach the Forms. *(FINDLAY enters.)*

FINDLAY: Hello again, Socrates and Phaedrus! How have you been spending your time down here—or should I say *up here*—in Hades?

SOCRATES: We've been talking with Ayer and Popper. They've been trying to convince Phaedrus that it's not the philosophers' fault he feels adrift.

Ayer says Phaedrus erred by asking a question that can't be answered meaningfully. And Popper says he missed a chance to build on the errors of others. In short: Ayer told him his question is meaningless whereas Popper told him it is indispensable.

FINDLAY: Then perhaps it's time I picked up the thread again . . .

PHAEDRUS: No—hold on! Before you all start talking about my problem again, I want you to understand what the problem *was*, the one I carried when I sailed from Piraeus. My question wasn't "What is that which is?"—that was just the *form* I gave it, to make myself understood by the philosophers in Miletus and Ephesus. My real question was: *What is this? (PHAEDRUS gestures in a wide, embracing motion.)*

(AYER, PLATO, POPPER, and KANT look at one another, perplexed. The stage begins to tremble. The lighting pulses in sync. A man's voice is heard.)

OSHO: Greetings, Phaedrus—and all of you. I am Osho's spirit.

Thank you for all your efforts—truly! Thank you for your question, Phaedrus. And thank you to the rest of you, for trying to answer what you *thought* was Phaedrus' question.

I read all your books—from beginning to end—when I was young. So many centuries. So many texts. So many concepts. And still—no answer. It's magnificent. You keep circling around being like cats before a closed door. But the door doesn't open inward. Or outward. There is no door. There is only *this* moment.

No system, no explanation, no ontology will give it to you. Consciousness doesn't arise from thinking. It arises when thinking *stops*. So I say: *STOP!* Stop philosophizing, stop analyzing, and be still. Be HERE.

All this talk of Forms, noumena, verification, dialectics. . .Why don't you laugh a little in stead, it helps. Is it really, all this talk, anything more than entertainment? Elegant entertainment, yes—but still. . . just *words*. You will never *find* truth through concepts. But you can experience it, right now, if you dare to let go of what you think you are.

(The lights stabilize. The walls stand still.)

PHAEDRUS: What. . . was *that*?

AYER: What absolute gobbledygook. I'm getting dizzy. *(An older man enters the room. It is EMMANUEL LEVINAS.)*

LEVINAS: That was a mystic, dear Ayer. Didn't you notice the walls shaking?

AYER: The walls shook? No. I saw nothing. I only heard a load of nonsense, worthy of Findlay at his foggiest. Who are you, anyway? Another of Hegel's disciples?

LEVINAS: I am Emmanuel Levinas. I sat in a German prisoner-of-war camp while my entire family—my wife's as well—was annihilated in other camps.

To me, shaking walls are nothing new. And the silence that Osho spoke of, yes, it is essential, but it is not enough. Being is not enough. Being is the satisfied grunt of a pig digesting its meal. Consciousness—real consciousness—doesn't arise in meditation, but in the encounter with the Other, with the face that demands: *See me. Take responsibility.*

Only through responsibility for the Other do we reach true being. So your question, Phaedrus—both versions of it—is a beginning. You are not the pig, grunting in the mud. But you've been looking in the wrong direction. You should have looked into the face. *(The walls and lights begin to tremble again.)*

OSHO: I hear you, Levinas. You speak of the Face. Of the Other. It's beautiful. It touches me, truly. But may I ask you something?

LEVINAS *(calmly, as the others recoil)*: Of course.

OSHO: Who is it that sees this face? Who is this human being who, the moment another face appears, becomes instantly responsible? The human being who still dreams, who loves today, what he hates tomorrow? Who speaks of truth, while still lying to himself?

You speak of responsibility. I speak of presence. You say: the human being *must*. I say: the human being *may, may* awaken. *May* grow still. *May* become clear. From *within*. It is not given, it is not inborn, but discovered. For one who still sleeps, even the holiest command is only an echo—a dream of goodness, cut loose from the real.

I don't reject the Other, Levinas. But I've seen many who spoke of love, who gazed into the face. And saw only their own reflection. *(The trembling fades. Light returns to normal.)*

LEVINAS: You speak of presence, Osho. Of wakefulness. Of an inner clarity that must come first. It sounds right. And it's hard to argue against something so serene. But I sense danger in your calm. Because the Face I speak of does not call to the *finished* human being, It calls precisely to the unfinished. To the one who is not ready, to the one who may never be.

Your words are beautiful, Osho. But they assume that the human being must first become himself before he can love, or act, or take responsibility. And I ask you: what happens while we wait?

(Pause. A spotlight comes on, revealing SIMONE WEIL, who has been silently present throughout.)

WEIL *(looking around at the assembled philosophers)*: Being. The Face. Presence. It all sounds . . . human. And therefore . . . insufficient.

What you say still rests on the idea that it is the human being who must act, awaken, love. But the human being—as he is—is a tyrant. Not out of malice, but by nature.

He wants to own, control, redeem, understand. Even when he says: *I love,* even in your ethics, Levinas, I hear *will.* Even in your transcendence, Osho, I hear *desire.* So the question is not: *How should we act toward the Other?* But rather: *How can we stop possessing everything*—including the Other? *(Pause.)*

There is only one movement that is not violent. Only one: To renounce. To let go. To de-create oneself. Not in resignation—but in an act of pure attention, so that the Other—maybe—can appear as real. Not seen, not felt, not grasped, but allowed. *(Long silence. No one dares to speak. Then FINDLAY steps forward, softly.)*

FINDLAY *(gently)*: And by "allowed," you mean . . . ?

WEIL: That the Other is permitted to exist without being overtaken by my will. That something—a human, a voice, a suffering—for once does not get reshaped by my thought, my love, my fear.

FINDLAY: So it's not about the Other being *recognized*?

WEIL: No. Recognition means that I have already placed the Other within my conceptual framework, and then it is no longer the Other. It is *me*, in disguise.

FINDLAY *(half to himself)*: A presence that is not mirrored . . . but permitted.

AYER *(to Popper, who doesn't respond)*: All this metaphysical self-erasure . . . If that isn't nonsense, I don't know what is.

WEIL *(to Findlay)*: Exactly. To let something *be*. Not out of resignation, but as the only true choice, once the will is freed from self and surrendered . . .

LEVINAS: Simone . . . In life I read you without sympathy. Without meeting you, as I should have. But now I understand: Your gaze pierces the will. And you're right: We take everything into possession. We see—and turn the seen into ours.

But . . . to give up everything, to step out, to become nothing—that too is a kind of power, an absoluteness the suffering face may not have time to wait for.

You say love is distance. I say: Love is wounded nearness, without guarantee. Not possession, but not absence either. For there, in the midst of my desire, my gaze, my guilt—there the Other speaks. Not as an ideal, not as a concept, but as a voice. A tremor in my freedom.

You would annihilate yourself, Simone. But I say: The Other needs me, not because I am good. But because I am there. *(A long silence. Then, from the audience, a calm woman's voice, smiling.)*

JACKIE *(from the shadows)*: Excuse me . . . but have you really forgotten me? *(A woman rises and walks onto the stage.)*

AYER: Pardon me, madam, but do we know each other? I haven't seen you at the general assembly.

JACKIE: You know my twin. I'm Jackie—Derrida's anima, the child Jacques was always trying to play, and never quite caught. But I was there, and surely you remember me after all the words I poured out over you while we were alive. I've lived many rich years writing about you all.

But let's not dwell on that. All of you—every single one of you—have done exactly what I expected. You've tried to *fix* meaning. With Forms, with Faces, with responsibility, with awakening, with suffering. But meaning, meaning *slips*. Every time we try to pin it down, it shifts. Every time we say "it's here," it moves over *there*.

Even your silence is a language. Even your suffering has syntax. And your ethics? It starts, like everything else, with a grammatical decision—with a *should*, instead of a . . . well, instead of what?

AYER: What on earth are you talking about?

JACKIE: Imagine a sentence: *He arrived late, but she smiled.* It seems clear, doesn't it? A delay. A reaction. Maybe forgiveness? But look more closely at it: Who is "he"? What does "late" mean? Five minutes, five years? And the smile? Triumph? Tenderness? Embarrassment?

The longer you stare at it, the more the edges blur. And if you try to explain the sentence, say: *He arrived late for dinner, but she smiled because she knew why,* you're merely restating the same ambiguity in different words.

To say that meaning slips isn't to say you're wrong. It's to say you're *human*—with language—and with the small despair that always comes with it. *(To PHAEDRUS)* And you, who asked the question—you're allowed to keep on asking. But know this: the answer will always be either a shoe too tight, or a language too loose. *(To the audience)* And if anyone asks who I really am—just say: I'm what remains when a text thinks it's finished. *(She sits quietly onstage.)*

WEIL: Who are you hiding from?

JACKIE *(hesitates)*: Hiding, hiding . . . perhaps I am. Am I like Jonah, fleeing the face of God? Though have you noticed, Simone, how peculiar the Hebrew phrasing is? Jonah doesn't flee *from* the face of God—he flees *to from the face of God* . . . That could make for a fine commentary . . .

(She looks at WEIL, who says nothing. Then, sadly) No one throws you overboard in language.

WEIL: Fear of water . . . . Is that what it's about, Jacques? I don't think so. I think something *drew* you, drew you to, not from. I think you need to reread Jonah, but also the Book of Genesis. Eve wasn't *threatened*. She was *tempted*. *(All fall silent. PHAEDRUS sits on the edge of the stage, hunched forward. SOCRATES approaches gently and sits beside him.)*

SOCRATES *(in an unusually gentle tone)*: You're trembling, friend. Is it the words that unsettle you?

PHAEDRUS: They pour over me, Socrates—like rain in a desert. But I'm not the soil that drinks. I'm the dust that washes away.

SOCRATES: And what is it that tears at you most?

PHAEDRUS: That they're all right, yet none of them touch me. They speak about me—about my longing, my question, my confusion. And yet I feel like an object—something they discuss . . . or better, like an enabler of their talk . . . does that make any sense, Socrates?

SOCRATES: Perhaps it's because they believe your question matters, but forget that the one who asks is alive . . . (*to himself*) But what do *I* do, in my questioning? *(Pause. Light lingers on Socrates. Then dims slowly, as a clock begins to tick and a leather couch rolls onstage alongside a coffee table with an ashtray. FREUD steps forward and addresses the audience like a professor lecturing to his students.)*

FREUD: Herr Phaedrus has asked: *What is that which is?* And the philosophers have responded with concepts of faces, ideals, unmaking, and deferral. They've offered him beautiful answers, some even uplifting. But Herr Phaedrus does not feel seen. And he is right.

What they do not understand—what I see—is that Herr Phaedrus's question does not arise from a blank consciousness. It arises from a body haunted by ghosts.

When a human asks *what is*, he is not seeking knowledge. He is seeking what he has lost. A mother, perhaps. A father, often. A feeling that once gave the world weight. He seeks because something no longer responds.

We do not desire *truth*. We desire to recognize something we once loved—and lost. Philosophers call it *Being*. I call it: the repetition of loss.

When Plato speaks of Forms, when Jackie dances with meaning, when Weil grieves with the grieving, they repeat themselves, again and again, to avoid feeling the void where love once spoke without words. *(Turning to PHAEDRUS)* And you, Herr Phaedrus—you sailed the Aegean in search of a voice that would not betray what you felt. Your father's voice, your mother's—or something from before they were? But, in any case, what you *felt* was already a construction, a shield, a defense. (*(Freud smiles dryly.)* That's nothing to be ashamed of. We all depend on illusions. The only problem arises when we call them *truth*.

So my answer is not an answer. It is a suggestion: Look at what repeats. Look at what you return to. Look at the words you use when you are most afraid. There you will find your reality. Not what *is*. But what you cannot let go. *(Freud lays his cigar in the ashtray and disappears into darkness without looking back. A distant rumble is heard. SOCRATES sits on the edge of the stage with his face in his hands. MARX sweeps aside the curtain and enters, unmistakable with his beard and broad brow.)*

MARX *(dryly)*: All very interesting, moving, even. Freud's concepts are like the oxygen of thought—we breathe them without knowing it. *(He raises his voice, facing the audience)*

But I ask you: Who gets to breathe? *(Pause.)* PHAEDRUS asks: *What is that which is?* And all of you, great thinkers, have answered the same way: With theories. Assumptions. Words and more words. But what about:

Bread.

Hands.

Soil?

You discuss Being, while those who keep you alive dig the fields, bake the bread, and die without ever being allowed to ask such questions. Philosophy is not just blind to the body—as Dr. Freud so rightly pointed out. It is blind to *class*. The question PHAEDRUS asks—*What is that which is?*—is not universal. It is a luxury. It is asked by one who has time. By one who is not starving. By one not carried in other people's pockets.

Remove the body from thought, and you get idealism.

Remove labor from thought, and you get ideology.

And remove ownership from what is—and you call it Being.

I call it: theft. *(In the background, the rumble grows louder. There's a crackling, like a great fire.)*

So I do not ask: What is? I ask: *For whom?*

End of Act Two

Act Three

SOCRATES and PHAEDRUS sit beside the charred remains of the oak tree. They begin speaking in alternating monologues, disconnected. Like two minds drifting side by side, not quite meeting.

SOCRATES: What have I done? They called me a midwife—but what was it, exactly, that I helped into the world? A stream of words? An eternal repetition? A language that cannot fall silent?

How did it happen? I was merely a loyal citizen, doing my duty as best I could, cultivating the *logos* in the agora, going to war when the city called. And no man could rightly say I owed him anything. What went wrong?

PHAEDRUS: How could I ask that question? I knew what is—even if I couldn't put it into words. It wasn't philosophy or the words that betrayed what is. It was me. For some perverse reason, I fabricated that question when I set sail from Piraeus. Why? And the exile—did I bring that on myself? Why did I mock Demeter, a harmless old woman, worried for her daughter? (*with a sigh*) They said I mocked her. But it was worse. I mocked her love for Persephone. And I knew it. Deep down, I knew it.

SOCRATES (*still unaware of Phaedrus' words*): It was a good question, a good question, Phaedrus! So how could it lead to this? To all these dry twigs rubbing against each other without producing fire?

PHAEDRUS (*half to himself*): Without producing fire? (*smiles at Socrates and now speaks to him.*) There was fire in the end, Socrates . . . may I tell you something strange?

SOCRATES: Of course, my friend.

PHAEDRUS: Once, before I mocked Demeter, I had an experience. I was walking toward Eleusis, my mind full of gloom. There were rumors of a storm in the Euripus Strait, and I feared one of my grain shipments from Euboea had gone down. I thought I was facing ruin. But as I walked, suddenly it came to me: *But you are loved! And you have always been loved, even before your mother bore you.* It was like a tidal wave, like an invasion. A certainty more vivid than any other I have known.

I was so happy.

SOCRATES: You never told me this.

PHAEDRUS: No . . . Do you know what happened next?

SOCRATES: Tell me.

PHAEDRUS: A little farther on the road, I met a small boy, maybe eight or nine years old. I don't know what he was doing there alone. But I felt a powerfull urge to tell him what I now knew. So I called to him, and when he ran over to me, I told him that he was loved. Do you know what he did, Socrates?

SOCRATES: No?

PHAEDRUS: He ran, Socrates—he ran away from me as if I had shouted at him in rage.

SOCRATES: And when you returned to Athens, you refrained from telling your friends about your experience . . . Was that because of the boy's reaction?

PHAEDRUS: No. Actually, I told others on the road to Eleusis. Some reacted coldly, others kindly—"Good for you!" one said. And one old woman patted my hand and smiled at me, gently. No . . . I don't really know why I didn't tell you about it, it wasn't the boy . . . When I got home, I learned the storm hadn't taken my ships after all, and then I got busy. Brokers, accounts, you know. And then, I suppose, I forgot . . .

SOCRATES: You forgot that you were loved—loved before your mother bore you?

PHAEDRUS: No. . . that's not quite believable, is it? How can you forget something like that?

SOCRATES: But now you've told me.

PHAEDRUS: Yes. Thank you for listening, Socrates. It needed to be told . . .

SOCRATES: No—I think *you* needed to tell it, Phaedrus. Will you go back to the road to Eleusis now?

PHAEDRUS: Should I? *Must* I? Simone Weil would probably say yes. Or would she? . . . And I can still feel the force that drove me to call out to that boy. It was as if all of me was in that call. As if I *became* myself in calling . . .

SOCRATES: Do you wish you could stay in that call forever? Would you wish to remain in that calling all the time?

PHAEDRUS: Can I? I *could*, I suppose. But do I dare? . . . Maybe there's another way: On the way home from Eleusis I also met a father and his son. The father looked so stern that I didn't dare tell them about my experience. But I smiled at the boy. And as I smiled, I saw him—not just his face, but *him*, behind the little hardened warrior-face he had put on for his father's benefit. And when he saw my smile and what it knew about him, he felt *seen*—seen in a way he never had been seen before, I think . . . (*a* *pause*) And maybe, Socrates . . . maybe that's enough. If I won't go around proclaiming that we are loved, then maybe I can smile at boys, at men, at women on the street. And in that smile pass on what was given to me.

SOCRATES: Maybe, Phaedrus. I guess you'll find out.

PHAEDRUS: Yes, maybe . . . Where do we go from here, Socrates?

SOCRATES: Do we have to go anywhere? Why not just lie back and admire the clouds drifting across the sky?

PHAEDRUS: That would get boring.

SOCRATES: So what? Is that a problem? And maybe it won't stay boring. Maybe there's something behind boredom, just like there was something behind your fear of financial ruin. Maybe one can go *through* it . . .

PHAEDRUS: Now you sound like that Osho guy.

SOCRATES: Except Osho had even more words than I do. (*They smile at each other again.*) No, the answer probably isn't in boredom. Hmm . . . Why do you think *they* kept going?

PHAEDRUS: Who kept going with what?

SOCRATES: The philosophers—sending new words after the old ones, as Osho said—generation after generation, lifetime after lifetime, day after day, in Königsberg and Oxford, whatever those places are . . .

PHAEDRUS: Not because they wanted to be professors—that is, tutors for the upper class's dim-witted sons.

SOCRATES: No, not even Ayer, I think. There was something else driving them . . .

PHAEDRUS: Kant's "metaphysical longing"? That we can't help but ask the question?

SOCRATES: Because we are . . . *voces timidae in deserto clamantes*, to paraphrase a text from another tradition?

PHAEDRUS: Yes, maybe. Because we seek what I found that moment on the road to Eleusis? Because we seek comfort, because that moment never lasts—because it may never come, even though we know it is there. Because we dare not hold on to it when it *does* come? Because it is here all the time, as Osho would claim . . . Because our misery over our all-consuming ignorance is so great that we are willing to do anything to soothe it?

SOCRATES: Or because there really *is* another place we're meant to long for, as the man with the schoolbag full of student papers and cousin Plato claimed . . .

PHAEDRUS: After which they spent the next many years marking student papers and writing long stories about you, Socrates.

SOCRATES: Yes, but let's stay with the serious bit. Maybe that place has something to do with the experience you had on the way to Eleusis. Maybe it's not only a place that *calls*, like love does, but also a place we *fear*. As we fear being loved—truly loved—as we were loved before our mothers loved us?

PHAEDRUS: . . . *voces clamantes* . . .

SOCRATES: And what are *we*, the two of us, as we sit here chewing on the same old thoughts? Maybe we should get on with something useful . . . What say we start that conversation Plato wrote down in *Phaedrus*?

PHAEDRUS: Okay, Socrates, let's do that. (*PHAEDRUS stands and walks around the stage*) . . .

Phew, that was a tough morning! Maybe a short walk outside the city walls, where birdsong replaces the boom of men's voices, can clear my head. . . Wait, who is that lying under the oak tree? He's calling out to me. *(PHAEDRUS approaches the man).*

Finis

Soft Words and Dry Thoughts

First

Helen Keller writes: *How shall I write about my mother? She is so near to me that it almost seems indelicate to speak of her.*

But isn't it precisely love that makes true writing possible?

Writing becomes indelicate, surely, only when we can no longer look upon the other with loving eyes.

I once owned a book by the parish priest Peder Winsløw of Præstø, published a few years before his death in 1750. Before I sold it, I wondered what bound its scattered texts together—what made them a *book*.

Perhaps the unity was nothing more than Peder's need to whisper across Præstø Fjord: *this matters.*

Closer to the Ground

Lives

THE SISTERS
Two small girls: one refined, lonely, afraid of the world.
Her sister: greedy and closed, already a part of it.

THE BELL
Out on the street a boy stands ringing his bicycle bell.
A little way off, his father bends over his little sister's bicycle.
The boy has no idea what's going on inside him,
and perhaps he'll never be allowed to find out.

UNDER THE OTHER'S GAZE
Under the foolish patient's severe gaze, the seasoned doctor recoils.
Like a plant in its pot, each of us struggles to reconcile what we later discover about ourselves
with the constraints we learned to impose on ourselves as children,
to secure what we needed then.

IN THE BROTHER'S SHADOW
In the garden, the sick boy's brother blasts his outrage through the boombox.
Why is it so hard for me to feel sorry for him?

THE HAND
The child raises her hand as if to speak, then lowers it again. Her eyes follow the adults' conversation.
A future silence takes root here.

DEPENDENCE
"She can't do without me," said the loud man about his wife.
She smiled modestly.

A DESIRE FULFILLED
"I hate dependence!" said the teacher.
Ten years later his eyes lit up when his wife entered the room.
He had been paralyzed from the neck down for three years.

THE HOUSE'S SECRET
Poul grew up in his parents' house and stayed there after they died.
Behind the wallpaper, mold spread.
Poul died at fifty-nine, and no one wondered.
As his friend Per said, "We always thought
he was something of a weakling."

Everyday Life, Seen from Within

DOES SHE SEE ME?
In the morning I spoon the grains for porridge into the pot. After each spoonful of spelt, I inspect the pot for small stones; the buckwheat I scoop without inspection. Once the porridge is on the stove, I take the plates down from the cabinet and run my fingers carefully along their insides to make sure there's no lime residue.

Every day I wonder how the woman across the street makes sense of my rituals.

TABOO
The last two spoonfuls of porridge are eaten with sugar. The sugar must melt from the porridge's moisture but must not mix with the melted butter. Otherwise the sugar will contaminate the sugar-free regions and dilute the pleasure of both the sugared and the unsugared porridge.

YOU AND ME AND WE TWO
The turd drops into the bowl.
"Thanks for your cooperation!" I say.

THE HIDDEN LONGING
When I open the TV listings, I discover a hope I didn't know I carried. Only when I see that there's nothing to watch tonight do I feel the longing. The hope was there, just out of sight, and now it announces itself as sorrow.

CHANGE
I wear button-up cardigans now.
Am I a new Jacob?
Nah.
It's the cardigan that has changed.

ARE YOU STILL HERE?
I visit the cemetery every day. It's to remind myself of life's transience, I say.
But maybe it's to convince myself that the dead are still there.

MUTUAL CONSIDERATION
The water pressure in the old house is low, so we avoid using water in the kitchen when the other is in the shower. Fifteen years later we discover that the kitchen water runs through an entirely separate pipe system.

BODY VS. SOUL
My wife is worked up over the dinner for her boss. I'm standing over the toilet, trimming my nails. I think: *As annoying as she is, she deserves a few clippings on the floor.*
And my body leans a little farther over the bowl.

HIDDEN DESIRE
One of our former cleaning ladies left a fork behind. Every time I use it, a memory of sexual fantasies drifts through me.
I never set the table with that fork when my wife is home. That would be like waving my infidelity under her nose.

Gently

DO MICE HAVE BLOOD?
"Do mice have blood?" he asks across the coffee.
She laughs, and his face closes.
"Were you really hurt when I laughed?' she asks, surprised. He smiles back, lovingly.

CARE
We look after each other: I think she should see a doctor about her cough, she thinks I should see one about my sore knee.
We'll see.

THE SMILE
On the platform I pass a man with his little daughter. He seeks my gaze as he embraces her. A smile passes through me, unplanned, and reaches him.
Later I meet them again. He seeks my gaze once more. Now I'm elsewhere; the smile must be forced. I see his need—yet give him only my own smile.

AUTUMN
Arriving at the summer house, I'm near tears at the coming of autumn.
When I've finished closing up for the winter, I notice that the sorrow is already gone.
Would I die of grief if the projects didn't exist?

THE FIRST TOOTH

After my first tooth extraction, I walked through the cemetery where my parents lie.
At their grave, I pressed the tooth into the turf.

WELCOME!

The recurring happy thought: How sad that this can't go on. And at the same time, when the body makes, on its own, a small turn to the left or to the right—unexpected, uncontrolled—and something opens downward: *Is it now? Welcome!*

On Some Shared Conditions: The Near

Small Imbalances

BODY CONSCIENCE
The alarm rings. I've slept badly and decide to stay home. But I can't fall asleep again.
You know that feeling?

THE MORNING BREAK
Aah! Now for rye bread with sharp cheese and strong coffee with plenty of sugar and milk.
The first bite matches the first sip perfectly. But why are there always two bites of cheese sandwich left when the cup is empty?

BEHIND ME
I simply can't stand people talking behind me.
And yet I take every chance I get to walk behind people talking together.

ON THE BUS
A large woman with a Middle Eastern look pushes her way firmly down the crowded aisle. *Fucking ***!* I think from my seat in the back.
A younger man glares at her. *Damn racist!* I think.

ON THE TRAIN

A young woman with loud music in her headphones sits down across from me.
I move farther down the car.
I could have asked her to turn it down.
But I'd rather punish her for my desire.

RETURN

Inside *Phew, it's hot, the shoe pinches, I'm hungry, why is she so irritating?* is beauty.
Otherwise I wouldn't have come back.

BEHOLD THE HUMAN!

On the bus a young woman tells a young man, laughing, that her mother used to beat her when she kept falling as a child.
Three stops later they get off,
and I turn in my seat to see what such a woman looks like.

THE GIFT

She thanked me for my present with a radiant smile,
and I walked away feeling guilty.

Original Sin

THE HIERARCHY OF GUILT
Yesterday I gave the liver-sick beggar outside the grocery store the loaf of bread I had just bought. I went back in and bought another one. When I came out again, I gave him five hundred kroner.
Three steps later it struck me that I hadn't invited him home with me.
Lately I wake every morning in guilt: guilt for not having fixed the kitchen cabinet, guilt for buying more books than I had promised, guilt for not calling Uncle Henrik.
But not for the beggar.

ENDURANCE
To see my guilt, I must endure it.
Can I endure the starving child on the evening news?
No. And that I must live with.

Little Cruelties

TOGETHER

At the house meeting Søren says once again that he and Sanne will be moving out of the collective.

I say across the table to Sanne that I hope they stay. I'm looking forward to our seeing each other through for the rest of our lives.

Søren's little brother screamed the whole way as they drove him to hospice.

FILIAL LOVE

Every evening at eight I call my mother.

One night she's upset about the Middle East. I distract her with a question about our first house; we talk about childhood, youth, memories.

When she starts to ramble, I tie a thread back to the Middle East —and hear myself think: *No. You're not doing this.*

The Arc of Life

1

Small children love getting a bandage.
When do we lose that source of comfort?

2

The grandchild says contentedly, “My grandpa’s old, so he doesn’t use soap. But girls do.”
On the way to opposites: girl–boy, young–old.

3

We were four in the back seat of the Volkswagen; as the oldest I had to keep my elbows in.
Now I get carsick on the bus whenever my wife’s elbow happens to rest against my hip.

4

“Yuck!” says the teenage son as they pass an elderly couple kissing.
“Well,” says the father.

5

Can you tear yourself apart? he asked himself.
The answer came many years later.

6
He lost his desire at fifty.
After that he could smile at the young women.

7
She still says "Come on!" and "So what?" now and then,
in just the same way she did in his childhood.
But now she no longer knows what it is that annoys her.

8
There's nothing I have to do.
Not even nothing.

Attention

ATTENTION 01
You can't just see a door.
It's always either a beautiful door or an ugly one.
Or something in between.

ATTENTION 02
The boy talks and talks.
Grandmother walks beside him, holding the phone.

ATTENTION 03
"Shhh!" we say to each other in turn as we walk through the woods.
"Now we're going to listen to the birds."

ATTENTION 04
It isn't the traffic outside my window that disturbs my reading.
It's my irritation with it.

ATTENTION 05
She reacted to his gaze as if no one had ever seen her before.
. . . Had he smiled at her?

Small Things?

JOB ANNO 2025
I've developed psoriasis. It itches so badly I can't sleep at night, and now and then the terrifying image appears of Job sitting in the ashes, scraping his sores with a potsherd.
But the worst of it is that I've become one of those people who leave marks on everything with the thick cream they rub on themselves.

DAMN!
The performance is canceled.
The lab results came back normal.

WHO I AM?
Look! I'm walking up the stairs to the houses.
Not the ones to the apartment blocks.

EVEN AMONG BROTHERS
My brother notices a Danish edition of *Critique of Pure Reason* on my desk and asks, "Do you read Kant in translation?"
I reply, "Only for the notes."

THE UNDERLINING
My pen hesitates for a moment over the page.
I think it's wondering what the next reader of this book will think of its owner if I underline this sentence.

The Gift of Loneliness

THE GIFT OF LONELINESS
To see you *as*.
To know that you're mine.
That is the gift of loneliness.

Under the Light of Screens

PODIUMS FOR ALL

Becoming a teacher was once a legitimate way to gain attention.
Today we are all teachers—the platforms hand out podiums.

PLACE OF RESIDENCE

For most of us, the internet-based matrix is just as frightening as the life we once lived in huts and fields.
The present moment is, after all, the only livable place to stay.

STILL PLAYING

Boys still play football.
It takes so little:
A ball, two goals, and a chair for the photographer.

OH—RIGHT . . .

When we're too tired to do anything, we're left to ourselves.
Oh—right . . .

IN THE LIGHT

He rides his bike up the shaded road toward the field, glowing in sunlight.
He slows down and takes a picture.

On Some Shared Conditions: Universals

Seven Theses on Love

FIRST THESIS
Love cannot speak.
Therefore it cannot do without mind and flesh.

SECOND THESIS
Love knows no gender.
That makes many relations possible.

THIRD THESIS
Everything changes, yet remains unchanged:
Ambivalence is love's raw material.

FOURTH THESIS
Love is objective.
It sees everything and endures everything.

FIFTH THESIS
Love was inherent in the first atom of carbon.

SIXTH THESIS
The expression of love is small quarrels.

SEVENTH THESIS
Love is a solitary task.

Three Reflections on the Commandment

THE COMMANDMENT AND THE HUMAN

The commandment of love has, through history, inspired millions despite others' indifference and resistance.
That must say something about humankind
—and perhaps also about the Commandment itself?

THE GIFT AND THE BURDEN

In the welfare state, the rich man cannot give away all he owns and follow Jesus.
The gift becomes a burden.

SERVICE AND SYSTEM

In modern working life we do everything for others—production, service, administration.
Without their needs our projects lose meaning.
At the same time we act almost cut off from what others do for us; if they stopped, we would go on until we died of hunger. Or until the supply of raw materials ceased.
What happens when we realize this?

Familiar Splits

THE TWOFOLD I

We live a contradiction between the conviction that I Am and the belief that I am a somatic, social, and psychic construction.

WHO WILL FOLLOW THE COFFIN?

The modern human sciences dissolve inner dualities into a continuum of natural processes.
Instead of body–soul, telos–reason, or good–evil, everything is described in physiological, evolutionary, or cognitive terms.
Thus we lose the image of the human as torn between forces, and attention shifts to explainable mechanisms.

THE GAZE—FROM WHERE?

Late modernity is the age of the externally directed subject.
For Descartes, the rule was: what I perceive clearly and distinctly is true.
Today it is often: what can be seen and approved by others is real.

THE SPACES BETWEEN

That we can talk about what it is like to be "me" shows precisely that much of the time we do not feel ourselves.
If we felt ourselves all the time, we would not know what it is to miss that sensation.

The Common Ground

OUTER/INNER

As self-evident as it is that "Hans fell because Grethe pushed him," so obscure is it why I fall into one mood or another.
My outer world, it seems, is far more transparent than my inner one.

HOW DO YOU KNOW?

We are born without knowing that we have a liver and kidneys. In fact, we would live our whole lives without knowing we were equipped with a liver and kidneys were it not for our embedding in a society that makes knowledge of livers and kidneys available to us.

THE BURDEN OF PERSPECTIVE

All knowledge is perspectival—even ours.
That insight is one we all struggle with.

THE GREAT REDISTRIBUTION

None of us—rich or poor, learned or unlearned—knows what This is about.
The only thing we know is This.
What This rests in, if anything, we do not know.

IN THE WIND—TOGETHER

The wind howls around my warm winter coat.
A man walking the other way clutches his short jacket.
Between us, a quick grin.

Leaves and the Wind

MEMENTO I
Without the wind's pull on the leaf, the trunk does not move.

THEY WERE ALLOWED TO STAND
The trees bend over the road.
In the wind they curtsey, grateful for the axe's mercy.

AUTUMN
Flocks of birds are flung above the treetops
while a carpet of brown leaves settles beneath the water in the canals.
A few drakes still try their luck.

SPECIES IDENTIFICATION
Birch leaves fall onto the road.
No two are alike.
I wonder if pine needles differ too?

MEMENTO II
The city's sounds are flayed by the wind.

THE CHANGING OF THE WINDS

There isn't one wind, but many:
the one that now ripples the pear tree's leaves
was rushing through the beech a moment ago.
And the little breeze that, as I write this, makes me consider putting on my jacket
is not the same as the one stirring the pear tree's leaves.
So why do we say, *There's a strong northwesterly today, isn't there?*
or, *The city's sounds are flayed by the wind?*

BEDCLOTHES

A storm blows between my toes.
The quilt is too short.

On Society, Seen from Within

Social structure

DANISH HISTORY
Behind the tree the castle glimmers
The pane encloses the curve of the spine
The park mirrors the weight of the clay.

A PROVINCIAL TOWN, 1962
Through the open window I heard Preben say, "But I don't want to play with him!" and his mother reply, "But you must!"
My grandfather was the director of the factory where Preben's father worked. I can picture him jovially telling the story about his grandson, visiting from the capital.
But I can't see whether Preben's father had his cap in his hand.

CAREER GUIDANCE, 1962
"The only thing that would make me sad," their mother said, "is if any of you wants to be a soldier or a priest."
She forgot to add agricultural laborer, chimney sweep, and ambulance driver.

IN A SUBURB, 2025
"May I sit here?" asks the woman at the bus shelter.
She's missing three front teeth.

Social Change

SOCIAL MOBILITY

In the fifties, it was very hard for a professor's child to become a bricklayer.
Fortunately, it's much easier today.

CAN THERE BE TRUTH IN A POOR EXCUSE?

In the mass society, it is not enough for the individual, in the moment, to do what needs to be done: help the old woman with her groceries, give the beggar a meal, tell the passengers standing at the front of the bus to move back so more can enter. What needs to be done is more complex than what the person on the spot can accomplish.
In the welfare state, most care must pass through systems. Immediacy is rarely sufficient.

THE INNER CHEEK

Two thousand years ago, it was about receiving what came from without—turning the other cheek.
Today, it's about receiving what comes from within.

UNBELIEVABLE!

Imagine that there was a time when no one missed cities, summer houses, or being transgender.
Unfassbar!

On the Sciences, Seen from Without

Macro

THE VIEW FROM WITHOUT
A major virtue of science (and of thinking, and of language) is that it can establish a place from which one may look at the world, and at oneself within it, less colored by one's own egocentricity.
The danger is that one may be tempted to stay in that place.

THE VIEW FROM WITHIN
The mystics' states of consciousness point to what is real. They are not what is real.
Outside the meditation hall, I wait patiently.

THE VIEW FROM BELOW
"A pipe—is it only metal if it's real?" the boy asks his mother.
(She answered: "No, it can also be plastic.")

Meso

TIME

"Time" arises from the question *What is time?* just as the three physical concepts of time (in thermodynamics, relativity, and quantum mechanics) arise within their respective theoretical structures.
So it's perfectly fine that you're bored while my time flies.

SPACE

Heidegger exposed the ontological limitation of the Cartesian model of space but overlooked the fact that its very abstraction had already, by 1927, proven unsurpassed in technological usefulness—and that prior theoretical study of the model is a condition for the application of its techniques. In this case, *Vorhandenheit* precedes *Zuhandenheit*.
What would a model of space look like that spanned both philosophical and technological reality?

LIFE

Aha! Biologists cannot agree on what life is. A significant minority holds that "life" doesn't exist.
Good to know for the likes of us mortals!

Micro

SCIENTIFIC TALK

Psychodynamic, sociological, evolutionary, and economic explanations may offer comfort:
Ah, that's *why I do it—so there's nothing seriously wrong with me. Nothing I must take an existential stand on?*
Do the human sciences, then, share responsibility for the soothing chatter that everyday life overflows with?

LOVE OF TRUTH WITHOUT A LOVER

A philosophy of the self that does not begin from the one who thinks reduces the mystery of the self to a technical problem.
Yep. That's a tempting option.

FREE WILL?

Parts of the social sciences and philosophy operate with the notion of free will.
Where do they get it from?

After the Soul

WHO ARE WE?
Naturalism's metapsychological trump card is this:
that we can neither predict what we will do in unfamiliar situations nor explain why we acted as we did.

THE OPEN SYSTEM
When the ball is put into play, the muscle fibers obey the law of energy conservation in closed systems.
But it's the gaze on the scoreboard that creates the energy.

EVOLUTIONARY PSYCHOLOGY
Evolutionary psychology comforts us with the thought that the tiger's ferocity has a purpose.
But Eichmann had no stripes.

THE PURPOSE OF CONSCIOUSNESS
Why should it count against the existence of consciousness that it serves no purpose?
That it is "superfluous"?
Who decided what its "purpose" was to be?

SELF-DECEPTION AND THE SEARCH FOR TRUTH

For Robert Trivers, the interesting thing is that we, as a species, evolved the capacity to deceive ourselves—allegedly because it makes us better at deceiving others.

But that doesn't surprise me.

If self-deception promotes survival, then of course we developed it.

The truly surprising thing, in that case, is the opposite: that we developed the capacity—and perhaps even the urge—to seek truth, whatever the cost.

How is that possible?

THE UNCONSCIOUS

To call something *"the unconscious"*—or worse: *"the cognitive unconscious"*—is misleading.

"Unconscious" is not a substance but a property.

You must first know what you're talking about before you can say whether it's conscious or not.

Unless you want to let it hide?

IS SOMETHING MISSING?

Present day psychology textbooks sketch theories of the self as a functional unit.

But isn't what's interesting about the self precisely its dysfunctionality—all its inner contradictions?

Or was that the soul?

THE ASTONISHED MACHINE

The test of whether science can replace the human must surely be that the successor can produce something that surprises itself.

ESSAYS IN ME

ME 1
After many, many years, I finally have myself.
But I still don't have the change.

ME 2
Here I am, shut inside my consciousness.
My consciousness?
I never asked for it.

ME 3
I'm not that important—
or else I'm far more than I think.

ME 4
I'm an incomplete angel,
while other people are complete bastards.

ME 5
How easily I could have been someone else!
There were millions of sperm chasing my mother's egg.

ME 6
What can I be?
In *The Oxford Handbook of the Self*, there are forty different suggestions.

Dogmatically Speaking

THE HISTORY OF TRUTH
Truth first appeared in the experience *Yes! that's how it is!*
How truth was later banished into language, I don't know.
The banishment produced religions, philosophies, and sciences.
Yet truth keeps reappearing within the walls of those very institutions.
It's as if it refuses to stay exiled.

THE FLIGHT FROM THIS
We move into fictions, enemy images, philosophies, religions, addictions, and stories of almighty parents and benevolent saviors.
If we can't place a good, cozy, nourishing world beneath *This*, we place a hostile one.
Anything under *This* is better than nothing.

WHY, WHY, WHY—ALWAYS WHY!
Is the very question "*Why is there something rather than nothing?*" not misguided?
Something is—*This* is.
To ask *why?* is to search for a motive outside the world, outside what is created, and there the question has no addressee.
Whom would you ask?

FAITH AND SPEECH

It makes no sense to speak of God as creator or good.
It makes sense to *believe* in God as creator and good.
That language seems the same in speech and in prayer is an illusion.

WINSLOW'S WAGER

Is God good?
If I live as if God is good, I become gentler, more loving toward others.
That benefits everyone.
Whether I'm right or wrong, life is lived better—for me as well.
But if I live as if there were no good God, anxiety, sorrow, or anger take root in me; they burden those around me.
If I'm wrong, I've created needless suffering; if I'm right, it hasn't helped.
In any case, it's a better bargain for me and mine to live in trust of God's goodness.

THE RIGHT DIET

Why can candy, cigarettes, promotions, academic degrees, new projects, a new lover, new clothes, or a new car never satisfy?
Because there is something else that can—and that something else is not a trip to Thailand.

PRAYER AND SURRENDER

Prayer is the willing (self-aware) surrender to what is.

It is not an *expression* of willing surrender—it *is* the willing surrender itself.

Hence prayer can take many forms.

SLOW SILENCE

Faith lives in silence and in slowness.

But not in every slow silence.

Faith is a gift, each time.

Longings

THE SUMMER HOUSE'S SECOND VOICE

A few days into my solitude at the summer house, where I have unlimited access to myself, a longing for something else stirs in me.

In the early years I would rush back to the city the moment that restlessness—that veil over longing—arose.

Now I just turn on the radio.

BETWEEN DALGAS BOULEVARD AND ÅLHOLM SQUARE

For several days I've had to stay indoors.

In the afternoons I find myself longing for the stretch along Roskildevej, where I've been forced to take my walks lately.

It surprises me—a major thoroughfare at rush hour?

Why not Frederiksberg Gardens or Søndermarken, where I used to walk before arthritis set limits?

Then I realize that the longing isn't for the places, but for the release that comes when the projects let go.

It's myself I long for—on Roskildevej between Dalgas Boulevard and Ålholm Square.

BETWEEN LONGING AND GRIEF

You can long for what you think you can regain.

Longing for what you know is lost forever—that's grief.

But you can also long for something you don't yet know what is.

THE EXPRESSION OF LONGING

It's tempting to see cruise ships as the expression of longing.
From there the language slides easily into familiar tracks:
Is the real object of that longing enchantment? The small child's ecstasy at contact with the physical? God? . . .
Can we let go of language?
Walk, with the puppy's gaze, along the pier's string of pearls?

WRONG ADDRESSEE

One morning a questionnaire from *Who's Who* lay on his desk. After spending the day, in a rush of happiness, embellishing his CV, he discovered that the cover letter was addressed to his father.

HUMAN LONGING

Karen Horney, Simone Weil, and C. S. Lewis each, in their own way, showed how we go astray in our longing.
Like the Church Fathers, they couldn't resist naming its goal.
Jesus and the Buddha smile encouragingly from their respective heavens.

(POST)MODERN LONGING

It's striking that we seek out reality-distorting representations—art, for example. Today it may be impossible to take a photograph without the device automatically doing something to the image: boosting color contrast, sharpening certain elements at the expense of others. Is this how our longing for Plato's Forms—that is, for God—now finds expression?

A BIT AMONG BYTES

In 1972 I read B. F. Skinner's *Beyond Freedom and Dignity* and wrote to Skinner asking to join his program at Harvard.

In my letter I wrote, among other things:

" . . . I am not only seeking an education which will make me fit for an academic career, but even more the establishment of a personal belief in the proposition 'I make sense' . . . ."

Ah yes—to be a bit among bytes, a chip among chips, a cog in a wheel—that *would* make sense!

And yet, it was truth that hid within that longing.

THE OLD DESIRE

Each time the doctor prescribes a new kind of medication, he feels the old desire awaken. He investigates: How should it be taken? When? What are the side effects?

Later he notes with care even the slightest change in body and mind, writing them down in a small black notebook.

And he fantasizes about increasing the dose.

In him rises the rush of hope: *Here is my Savior! This diuretic will carry me safely through coming storms. He is the rock upon which I can dance amid lightning and thunder.*

Later he writes in the black notebook: *Light dizziness, increased craving for sweets. Was it the same with the eye drops?*

GOD'S LONGING

To feel this—*that God longs for me*—can be a first step.
That may be what the addict experiences in the rush:
not that he *is* God, but that God longs for him.

Uncle P Speculates

LIFE EXPECTANCY
Life expectancy keeps rising.
Uncle P thinks: Maybe it's because God has noticed we still haven't gotten the message?

THE CITY
Uncle P, on an expedition:
A city is a continuous stretch of land where no one can pee in peace.

THE BOYS
One boy sits bent over his phone, body turned toward his friend as if to confide something important.
The other sits waiting, gaze locked.
The confidence never comes.
Uncle P thinks he's probably one of those boys who, as men, interrupt every other sentence with a *uh-uh-uh . . . let me see.*
But the other one—who will *he* become?

RECOGNITION
It's best to praise others for what they themselves wish to be praised for, Uncle thinks.
There are some things people do not wish to be praised for at all.

GOAL DISPLACEMENT

Uncle P counts his nighttime trips to the bathroom after cutting down on fluids.

Should I count the last one? he wonders.

After all, I never really fell back asleep afterward.

Uncle P wants the project to succeed, so he'll be sharper during the day.

But will he actually be sharper because the average number of nightly bathroom trips in his statistics is lower?

Grandpa Reminisces

Him and his body

THEN AND NOW
When I was young, I would skip down the stairs while flirting with the pretty girl beside me.
Today I have to focus all my attention on the steps beneath my hesitant feet.
Why did I never notice this was on its way?

DUE CARE
It's wrong to see the changes the body goes through with age as decay.
They're more like due care: the body preparing itself for death.
Not everyone gets to be hit by a car.

PLATO WOULD HAVE BEEN DELIGHTED
The advantage of glaucoma growing steadily darker is that things disappear and forms return.

AFTER THE OPERATION
From now on I only need to use my eye drops in the morning and evening.
My lunchtime visit to the medicine cabinet is cancelled.
A small sorrow blows through me.

NEW EXPERIENCES
I can no longer tell my charcoal-gray phone from my black desk, so I have to feel my way when I want to use it.
Exciting! An old sense opens up again.

HESITATION
In an unfamiliar situation, the body becomes cautious.
It's as if it asks each movement, each small turn of the head, each bending of a knee:
Do you really belong in this action?

BETWEEN THE FINGERS
After I've washed and dried my hands, there's still dampness between my fingers.
It didn't use to be there.

THE SOUND OF SILENCE
Silence is a sound.
Otherwise I couldn't hear it through my tinnitus.

MY SILENCE
The silence is *my* silence.
That's why the boys can play soccer in it.

Him and Others

MATURITY

My seven-year-old granddaughter doesn't get offended when I don't come when she calls.
But I get offended when she doesn't come when I call.
What's happened to me since then?

THE EVENING WALK

On my evening walk I exchange loving glances with the cow and scratch her forehead.
She doesn't know I've just eaten her calf.

ON WHOLEHEARTEDNESS

Isn't there something touching in itself about watching another person make an effort you wouldn't make yourself?
To do things in earnest.
To do things completely, with a whole heart.
Like a small child eating candy.

BEYOND THE SPECIES

The dog stood by the door and whimpered when its person went out.
There it stood.
We become responsible for those we make dependent on us—people as well as animals.
Why then does that responsibility feel smaller?

Him and his Future

MISTAKEN IDENTITY

I'm standing on the bed shaking out the duvet—but it was the sheet that was supposed to go out the window.
A small laugh. And a stab of fear.

THE FUTURE OF THE PAST

I'm now so old that what I experience—new places, for example—can no longer become the past.
Do you remember when we . . . is no longer a sentence that lies ahead.

THE TENSION OF LIFE

What is this discomfort that plagues the body before the day's projects begin . . . ?
Could it be the tension of life, finally making itself known?

REUNION

There is a memory of my grandmother in the slowness with which I now rise from low chairs.
We are reunited in old age.

MOVING ON

I'll move on. Perhaps into Heaven, perhaps into a horsefly. But I'll move on.

A Pause

Lord Almighty,
You who have created us and who shape us,
You who love us and care for us,
You who hold Your hand beneath us, and let us fall,
You without whom nothing is,
You whom no one and no word can grasp:
Thank You for today! Thank You for this moment!
Thank You that I am clean and sober!
Thank You for the people in my life,
those who are and those who were!
Your will be done, not mine!
May all that happens to me, and all that I can do,
be for the benefit and joy of other living beings!
Deliver me from my resentment and my envy!
Deliver me from my condemnation of other people
and my negative perception of them!
Deliver me from my sense of grievance!
Thank You!

Drier Waters

Words always give too much or too little of the world. That is one reason for disagreement between statements.

Philosophy tried to heal this by enforcing logical consistency—by insisting that nothing can be both A and not-A.

But perhaps it sought to mend the wrong wound. What we need is not only the purity of logic, but also intelligence in handling contradictions—both within and between texts.

In the Land of Projects—A Longish Story

THE PARADIGM

I sit down. After three minutes, I sense a bit more weight on my right hip than on my left. I shift in the chair and feel the imbalance disappear. That's the paradigm of a project.

BETWEEN PROJECTS

Before drinking my morning tea, I set the bag of dishwasher tablets in the middle of the kitchen counter. It helps me drink my tea in peace: the next project is defined. I don't have to remind myself to turn on the dishwasher when I'm done.

I could have opened the door of the machine as well, but that would have been too much. During the tea, I would have been reminded of an unfinished project.

THE PROJECT IN THE BODY

I get an idea while sitting on the bus. A project comes alive, but stops somewhere between the first spark and the making of a plan. I don't have the needed resources—no paper, no pencil. In the body, a faint vibration in the muscles; inside that, a holding of muscles and bowels; and in consciousness, a struggle to hold the idea, while new aspects crowd in: there's also this, and that, and . . .

A DISTURBANCE

My colleague enters my office as I'm in the middle of writing a particularly successful argument. He insists that I listen. When he leaves, I can't find my way back to the thread, and a strong anger rises in me. A growl runs through the body, a burning weight in the stomach—then the thought: *where am I, where was I going?*

THE UNEXPECTED RESULT

Is painting a picture or writing a poem a project? Yes, of course: lack/possibility, goal-setting, planning, execution, evaluation. But during the execution, the project structure may be suspended; that is, the work can move forward without feedback from the earlier phases of lack/possibility and goal-setting. In the final evaluation (*the poem is finished!*), one may then find that the result is unexpected. But that does not change the project character of the process.

I'M SORRY! I DIDN'T SEE YOU. . .

People can be resources in my projects. But they can also be irrelevant. "Sorry, I didn't see you," says the driver to the bleeding cyclist. And it's true. The cyclist simply wasn't part of his project.

PROJECTS LYING IN WAIT

I see the porridge needs five more minutes. In that time, I can answer Søren's email—maybe even clip my nails.

When the execution of one project is delayed, others take the opportunity to make use of me.

FREE TIME

Of course, the project manager does not spend all his time in projects.

On the long straight stretch between University Park and Vibenhus Roundabout, the projects release the driver's attention. He notices an anchor in the logo on a passing van and finds himself in a sunlit harbor with sailboats. From there he is moved to his grandparents' apartment, which once looked out over such a harbor.

Then he notices the waiting passenger at the bus stop, and the projects take hold again: speed, angle toward the curb, passengers getting off?

So the project manager has free time between projects.

INVOLUNTARY FREE TIME

Free time is the project manager's time outside the projects. Apart from sleep, it makes up only a small part of the considerable non-working time available to the inhabitants of the global North. That time is mostly filled with projects.

Free time appears—apart from sleep and boredom—only in small pieces: between projects, between stops.

Boredom is when no project catches hold.

Boredom is involuntary free time.

TIME AND OBSTACLES

On the bus to the dentist, I ask myself: *will I get there on time?* In the waiting room: *will it soon be my turn?* Afterwards: *when has an hour passed, so I can eat again?* In the perfect project, time doesn't appear—only the phases, joining seamlessly. In project-free awareness, time doesn't appear either—only shifting states of consciousness.

Time exists only in real projects, only by virtue of their obstacles.

WHO IS DISTURBED?

"Do not disturb me!" we say—not, "Do not interrupt the preparation of these accounts."

It is not the accounts that are disturbed. It is me.

A project can make me explode in rage: "Can I please get some peace!"

My resistance to being colonized by others' projects takes the form of resisting their entry into me.

More precisely, I should say: Do not disturb the execution of my project, or take its resources—here, my attention.

For surely I am not disturbed merely because the project is?

ON BEING SET IN MOTION

Like a lion in the sun, I lie here in bed and fill my mind with the body.

The body spreads out, fully content, except for the faintest tremor of reluctance to move.
But the ideas are spinning in the cortex, and soon they will force the body out of bed and over to the keyboard.
. . . But no, look—it is not the ideas that start the machine.
It is the project itself that seizes an idea from the cortex and drives the body to the keyboard.

THE PROJECT'S TAKE

The project says:
"I have the project manager; he doesn't have me. All resources and tools belong to me—he merely gathers them.
He is the steward of my estate."

. . . And I, I who sit here writing this book.
Who am I? Am I also a project manager?
Oh yes.
How could the book possibly write itself?

Tales of Varying Scope

Small

THE FLY

When I left the cottage the day before yesterday, a fly was struggling against the pane of a closed window.
I didn't help it.
This morning, when I came back, it was still lying in the window frame—alive.
I carried it outside;
it crept away weakly,
maybe nibbling algae from the wooden terrace.
Now it's gone, perhaps eaten by a passing blackbird.

THE CIA AGENT

In Havana, I stand on the sixth floor of a hotel with my binoculars, inspecting the communists' fortifications by the harbor.
It gives me a certain posture, a particular hand position, and a firmness in the inner feeling. I'm a CIA agent
—until my wife comes in from the bathroom
and blows the agent to bits.

SHARK MOUTHS

In my early forties, I realized that people on the street had shark mouths where I'd thought they had lips.
The trick—which I discovered ten or fifteen years later—was to smile at them.
Since then, the sharks have left me alone.

THE CANE CHAIR

A year and a half old, she wrestles with the little cane chair. There is only the chair and her body.
They must be coordinated before she can sit down. She struggles with the chair as she struggles with the rest of the world.
Adults know the world and know how to sit. She stands outside and fights to get in
or is it us who have shut ourselves out and now know only furniture?

THE RUINED CASTLE

"This is where I'll take my morning coffee every day for the rest of my life," I said,
standing at the ruined castle next to my new summer cottage, watching the sun dissolve the morning mist between the tall trees.
But I never had my coffee there again.

Medium

THE TOOTHACHE

We rarely remember the chains of thought we build on top of reactive feelings.
The moment believes itself unique: *I'm the only one who's ever woken with a toothache—and it's never happened to me before.*
Therefore this toothache belongs to world history, along with the Lisbon earthquake and the Second World War.

EPIPHANY AT THE BAR

At the Hall of Residence bar in London: an apparently sober first-year student offers to eat shit for a double whiskey.
The rest of us stare at him in disbelief.
Has he since managed to hold on to his epiphany—*It's just molecules! Don't you see, it's all just molecules?*

SUMMER RAIN

Today, for the first time this year, I hear the summer rain falling and recall the sound of rain one summer afternoon at Lundegården.
It is the only sound that remains from that childhood refuge.
As for smell, I only remember the attic and the cottage toilet—perhaps also the stairs down to the kitchen cellar—but that memory has slipped away.
How few memories, compared to the visual!
What would my idea of childhood be if it were based only on smell and sound?

THE QUARTO SERIES

He buys Modiano's *Romans* and discovers Gallimard's Quarto series.

The thin paper, the large type, the weight of the books—and his idea of the authors' solidity (Yourcenar, Duras).

He wants more.

In that wish lies a hunger for wholeness (*Habermas? I know him. I have them all—in German—right behind my desk chair*).

When he gives in and clicks on Gallimard's site, he sees that not only Yourcenar and Duras, but also Steinbeck, Margaret Mitchell, and Marcel Aymé are part of the series.

Salvation is postponed once again.

NO ONE HAD TOLD THEM THAT

There were sharp nails at the tips of their arrows,
and the blackbird had caught itself in a pile of brushwood.
But they couldn't kill it;
they couldn't bring themselves to do it,
even though their inability later confused them.
They were supposed to have been able to do it.
And they were supposed to have carried their dead prey home to the summer house in triumph,
celebrated by their younger sisters and their girlfriends,
and later praised for their courage and quick thinking
by proud parents.
Instead they walked home,
not in shame
but in a confusion that made it impossible to present the sequence of events
to the adults at the tea table.

Large

THE CIRCLE OF FAITH

If I am to convince myself that Jesus Christ died on the cross for the forgiveness of my sins, I must first believe that I deserve the forgiveness of my sins.
And so it goes in circles.

THE FACE OF FORGIVENESS

Do I want forgiveness?
What will I meet behind the injured one's angry eyes?
What happens to the world if the injured one lights it up with a smile?

THE DISENCHANTMENT OF THE WORLD

The world's disenchantment (Weber) isn't because science has succeeded in giving a rational explanation of the world.
It hasn't.
The disenchantment lies in the belief that such an explanation is possible.

Extra large

THE NARRATIVE SELF
"I'm not the kind of person who goes to group exercise classes!"
So the narrative self has causal power after all.

HAVING AND BEING
We say "my hand" and "my body."
Cancer patients can say "my cells."
When will we be able to say "my atoms"?

NARRATIVE AND UNDERSTANDING
In my story, I can either express an insight I already have, or reach a new one through the act of telling.
Does it ever happen that the two forms merge?

THE TRUE SELF
The true self reveals itself; it can't be expressed through a gender identity or a party uniform.

WHO?
The narrative self describes the world.
Who, did you say?

THE SMILE
What's in the smile?
Nothing, and therefore everything: forgiveness, recognition, being seen as who I really am.
The world is a good and safe place to be.

Mine—Another Long Story

The two-year-old girl and her mother sit on the bed, talking about her grandparents. The mother says, "Do you know that your grandfather is my father?" The girl flings herself backward on the bed and shouts, indignant: "My grandfather! *My* grandfather!"

At a class reunion, a red-haired woman told me that I had taken her virginity in 1967. I couldn't remember her. But I remember Stine from the June issue of *Cocktail* four years earlier—Stine with black fishnet stockings and coal-dark, angry eyes. Stine is mine. But I belong to the red-haired woman.

The young woman and I had exchanged smiles on the train to Tisvilde. When her boyfriend kissed her, I turned to the window and stared out, sulking.

My hand runs along the ten volumes of Habermas on my shelf. Habermas is mine. Perhaps the spines of Tore's copy of *Theorie des kommunikativen Handelns I–II* look more read than mine, but I own more of his works, and in any case, Habermas is mine.

My cousin Hans insists there was a henhouse where our grandparents' woodshed used to stand. He's so wrong I can feel it through my whole body.

What about "Tisvildeleje"? ("Tisvildeleje is a seaside town in North Zealand with fifteen hundred permanent residents.") No—the *concept* "Tisvildeleje" isn't mine.

But Tisvildeleje is. My Tisvildeleje is simply Tisvildeleje.

Only when I meet someone else's Tisvildeleje do I become aware of it as mine—because I know Tisvildeleje is *A*, while the other insists it is *B*. Only through such encounters may I realize that Tisvildeleje is *my* Tisvildeleje.

My wife comes home from the theater and tells me she met my cousin Francis and his wife, Odaline, during the intermission. A sharp pain shoots through my chest: those people are mine. *I* should have met them.

My sense of ownership branches into a fine web across the world. I met the sociologist Denise Kandel at a conference in 1971. She was—and still is—married to the future Nobel laureate Eric Kandel. So when I read his memoirs, I do so with a quiet intimacy: I *have* this Nobel laureate.

Many—perhaps most—of my *minenesses* can be negotiated. We can agree on which God our church will be built around, what kind of socialism our country should adopt, how our shared mother performed her role.

"All right then, X *is* . . . " I might say at the end of such a successful negotiation. But that's only in language. And perhaps it's something we pretend, for the peace between us. Because *mineness* can be negotiated *through* language, but it's established *before* language and belongs *there*.

Reflection shows me that others also have their *minenesses*, and that some of their referents overlap with mine. I know that my childhood overlapped with my sister Lilliane's, and I know too that she and I remember different episodes and assign different meanings in our tellable versions of the past. For instance, I remember vividly a loving remark Father made to Mother at Christmas dinner in 1962. It captured perfectly the essence of their relationship.

Lilliane doesn't remember it. After years of argument, we agreed that "we remember different things from our childhood." But in truth, the relationship between Father and Mother *was* as that remark expressed it. Whether Father actually made it that evening makes no difference.

Of course I can tell a Swedish tourist, "Tisvildeleje is a seaside town on the north coast of Zealand." But then it's not *my* Tisvildeleje I'm speaking of. My Tisvildeleje comes only in potential play if the Swede answers, "Oh yes, I used to go there as a child."

Mineness requires a stimulus to awaken. That Francis and Odaline are mine—and not my wife's—I realized only when I felt that sudden stab in my chest.

Is there a kind of hostility in *my* Tisvildeleje? Yes. Every time they subdivide one of the large summer-home properties, every time they tear down one of the fine old houses, every time they cut a tree in the wood, I seethe with anger. Whatever happens over in Rågeleje doesn't concern me.

Tisvildeleje isn't my only possession. What do all these possessions have in common—Stine from *Cocktail*, Francis and Odaline, the girl on the train, Habermas, Eric Kandel, my parents' marriage, and Tisvildeleje itself?

At first glance, nothing connects them—not the girl on the train and my parents' relationship, nor Stine and Habermas. What they share is that I will defend my right to them.

What does it mean to defend that right? It means I will defend my place as the one with the most privileged relation to, the deepest knowledge of, these people, objects, and situations. Their essences are, if not *in* me, then bound *to* me. For this reason I *have* them.

An example: Axel's beloved wife, Gräuben, has died. He often visits her grave. One day he meets a man his own age laying a flower there. "Who are you?" Axel asks.

The man explains that he was Gräuben's boyfriend all through high school—long before Axel knew her. He tells stories about Gräuben as a sixteen- to nineteen-year-old girl, and Axel listens, deeply moved. Here, no conflict arises. Not even when the man mentions their time as activists in the anti-nuclear movement. "What?" Axel exclaims. "Gräuben was a nuclear physicist—she worked at the nuclear research institution here in Copenhagen until they shut down the reactor in 2000!" There's nothing to fight about here—only something to rejoice in: another facet added to Axel's memory of his beloved.

Another situation: Axel meets Gräuben's longtime colleague, Ella. She tells him that many years into their marriage, Gräuben had an affair with their mutual friend Frederik. Axel never knew and is shaken. Will he fight about it? Only if he can't take it in and retreats into denial. Otherwise he may feel grief, anger at the no-longer-present Gräuben, perhaps even the urge to beat up Frederik. But he's not likely to fight over the fact. Even though Ella's revelation has added a new facet to Axel's picture of Gräuben.

A third situation: Axel is with Gräuben's sister, Helle.

They talk about Gräuben. Helle tells a story and ends it, saying, "But you probably can't understand that—you didn't know Gräuben that way." With that, she claims a version of Gräuben that includes something Axel doesn't know. Which means that she—not Axel—*has* Gräuben.

That could easily send Axel into a rage.

Everything that is mine (including my childhood) has boundaries I defend. And I meet others (like my cousin Hans) expecting them to cross those lines. Between people who know each other well, there are border agreements that prevent exhausting conflict. That's why such people seek each other out. Those with unresolved boundary disputes tend to avoid one another.

Can *mineness* be undone? Can I let go of ownership?

Yes, in the smile, in the sudden meeting, mineness may dissolve. Only to re-establish itself the next moment.

And in the sacramental community, the Church, the AA group, the party become *ours*. But over coffee after communion, after the Serenity Prayer, after the oath of allegiance, the church, the fellowship, the party become *mine* again.

Perhaps love reveals God's world by dissolving mineness. But can I really relinquish ownership once I've claimed it? Perhaps—if,

when faced with your claim on what is mine, I say, "Yes, that's how it is,"
and turn the other cheek.

On the Way to Me*

> I *and* me. I *feel* me—*that's two objects.*
> —Georg Christoph Lichtenberg

The point of departure must be *Me*—that is, the experience I have of myself. The problem is that I don't experience that *I*—that is, the "I"-experience—feels, thinks, or acts. Feelings, thoughts, and actions are things that occur alongside *Me.*

When I go from the living room into the kitchen to make coffee, there is no experience of "I am acting" in relation to my walking. I simply walk—that is, walking happens—and *I* go along.

If the feeling of me were the feeling of what it's like for me to eat mushrooms, to read Zahavi, and to play croquet, then the feeling of me would have to vary greatly from one activity to the next. Instead, through all three activities, there is the same feeling that is also there when I move from one activity to the next. And this something is *Me.* My self-experience is not stimulus-dependent; it's simply there.

The self-experience can shift from one person to another in my consciousness. One morning *I* woke and moved from being a tough young woman, opening the door to her apartment for her sweet, curly-haired, red-bearded husband and their two teenage daughters, to being mild, awake, and still *Me.*So in my consciousness *I* can be in two different persons.

Sometimes I dream that I take drugs. Then I wake up suddenly, relieved—thank God!—that I'm no longer an addict. So in dreams the feeling of *I* is connected with being active.

. . . Does the idea that *I act* come from the dream experience?

In a stab of shame—accompanied by involuntary movements (specifically a quick turn of the head from center to left and back again)—*I* vanish.

Who learns, if not a self? Who can walk, read, and speak French—but not yet Italian? Who is not yet demented? There *must* be an acting I!

Does it make sense to speak of an acting self that belongs to no one?

That is, to have an acting self and a sense of self, without the latter expressing the former?

But there *is* a self, because I can kill myself! What better proof could you ask for?

On this sea of ignorance, I usually comfort myself with one thing I know for certain: I did not create myself. That makes it possible to throw myself at the feet of the Creator, in the hope—in the trust—that He is benevolent.

. . . But do I really know this? Do I know that I did not create—or co-create—all this, including myself? For I now also know that the feeling of me, *Me,* is not me; it is not the agent that perhaps (or perhaps not) exists "within" me. And of what that agent—if it exists—may be co-responsible for, I have no idea.

Home at last: Me and Me*

I write: When I'm absorbed in a difficult task, or a gripping book or film, I am gone. But there's a problem with that sentence. The I in *When I'm absorbed in a difficult task, or a gripping book or film* is not the same I as the subject of *I am gone*. If it were, the problem-solving and the reading and the watching would stop when I disappeared. But they don't—they continue until the task is done or the film is over.

To distinguish the two referents, the I that can disappear will be written I* (and correspondingly me*, my*, mine*). The working I will be written I (me, my, mine).

I* am almost always present: when the heavy shadow lifts in the afternoon, and while dinner is prepared in an effortless flow I* am there. I* am there when boredom reigns. But I* am not always there. I* am absent in deep sleep, and gone when I'm overwhelmed by feelings—or when I'm wholly absorbed in a difficult task or a compelling book or film.

Try it yourself: multiply 27 by 13 in your head now.

. . .

I* was gone. Where were you*?

I am like a flashlight: my attention illuminates my surroundings. But I* am like a star: I* illuminate nothing, even though I* shine. And yet I* am not like a star, for there are countless stars, and I* am unique.

Things—even atoms—can be divided without end. I* cannot: I* either am, or am not.

The taste of the cookie fades in; I* do not—I* am either present or not.

Where is the boundary between me* and the rest of consciousness? It is not fluid: I* remain unchanged while everything else is in flux.

I* can be experienced as identical with my mood because there is almost always a mood present together with me*. But moods change by being observed (*Aha! I'm angry! Why?*). I* do not change by being observed.

When I* am present, I* am always present with something else—feelings, sensations, sensory impressions, thoughts. When I* am present, I* am always present with some part of me.

Can I and I* meet? We encounter each other constantly, but only I* am ever fully present. I always show only one side of myself. So perhaps we cannot meet.

So to call me* "the feeling of me", or "the feeling of self", is mistaken. I* am the same, while I am always changing. Thus I* am not the feeling of me, not the feeling of this ship sailing on the sea of ignorance.

But perhaps I* point to the ship, to the existence of the ship . . . or to something else?

Being and Knowing

Starting Points and Conditions

THE VERB *TO BE*
First, there are no things. *Is* is not.
Then comes a great explosion, and everything becomes.
But how can that be?

THE MEANING OF LIFE
Life should not be *given* meaning. Life is the very paradigm of the meaningful. If life is not meaningful to the one who lives it, then there is no meaning at all for the living.
What could such a meaning be?

IDOLATRY?
To ask, as Leibniz did, "Why is there something rather than nothing?" is to take the Creator's seat.
From a human perspective, the question is meaningless.
And to claim that God can answer it—is that not idolatry?

CREATEDNESS
"Createdness" is a human concept; snakes probably don't know it, and a limestone certainly doesn't.
From a human standpoint, the notion of createdness is natural, self-evident: humans see themselves create—thus when there is something, someone must have created it.
But how does it look from an animal's point of view? From a stone's?

BEYOND THE SENSES

There is that which we are made to sense directly—sounds, smells, sights.
And there is that which we can sense only through instruments—when we register rays beyond the limits of our senses.
But is there also something we will never be able to sense?

THE INSIDE

When we build a house and live in it, do we thereby also create an interior or an essence that is independent of us? Could it be that something in what we create exceeds our intentions in the act of creation?
. . . Might something similar have happened to God?

MATTER VERSUS FORM

It doesn't matter that what exists is biology—or physics. That changes nothing about experience, seen from within.
And since I am not God, I must necessarily see it from within.

THE BEGINNING OF THE GOOD

How do goodness, the longing for truth, and the sense of justice enter a material world?
They must have evolved from a more primitive foundation—something like "I'm full."

RECIPROCITY

What difference would an immortal soul make?

If the immortal soul does not exist, there is only a heap of matter, a social-chemical circulation. Thus nothing that can stand in mutual relation to the Creator.

But is that true?

Why should a heap of matter not have a mutual—if time-bound—relation to its maker?

Why should reciprocity require the immortality of both parties?

Do I cease to be related to my mother simply because she is no longer here?

CODA

Perhaps not only God but also I am the mystery.

Who I am, I know.

But what am I?

Perhaps the many failed attempts to explain myself serve only to heighten the mystery.

Perhaps that is their value—for without the explanations, the mystery itself might (perhaps) be forgotten.

. . . so perhaps the philosophical inquiry into the self is a form of prayer?

Forms of Surrender?

BEHIND THE LAW OF MATTER?

Is addiction an attempt to become pure nature—and, by submitting to the law of the substance (dose, timing, tolerance), to escape God's demand for surrender to what is?

Why not simply dissolve into *das Man*, like everyone else?

Perhaps because the law of the substance is so unyielding that God is glimpsed behind it.

"Surrender" to that law mimics surrender?

BEFORE PAIN HAD A CAUSE

Unexplained (causally unaccounted-for) pain or disability—like my current partial deafness—awakens curiosity and joy: *What is this? So this, too, is how being can be experienced?*

Pain embedded in a causal framework, by contrast, awakens concern. It is that concern, more than the pain itself, that leads to avoidance—taking a painkiller, or getting a hearing aid.

AMBIVALENCE

The pain in my knee says: "Yes, my leg is there."

And I reply: "Thank you."

Sometimes.

THE NEXT CHALLENGE

The mystics of antiquity—Plotinus, for instance—believed that to find Truth one must close off the senses.

In Christian mysticism, the task was to shut out everything except the thought of God.

Today we see the precondition as suspending our projects.

What obstacle will the future discover?

THE COMMON AND THE OWN

Why is it so important that reason can confirm faith, and that reason can justify action?

Reason is common, but faith is mine—like action.

THE EUCHARIST OF STATISTICS

Regression analysis is an attempt to glimpse God through the noise of data points—to see the eternal in the immediate.

IN GOD'S HANDS

I feel fragile, yes.

But what does that mean?

Abandoned to God's power?

HOW FAR CAN ONE GO?

Dietrich Bonhoeffer returned to Germany in 1939 to preach his version of the Christian message, fully aware that he was exposing himself to persecution.

In his diary he wrote:

> *It is remarkable that I am never fully aware of the motives behind any of my decisions. Is that a sign of confusion, of inner dishonesty? Or is it a sign that we are led without knowing it—or perhaps both?* (Metaxas, *Bonhoeffer*, p. 336)

In 1943 he was imprisoned; on April 8, 1945, he was sentenced to death and hanged the next day.

So far can one go without knowing why one does what one does. How far, I wonder, can one go if one *does* know?

On Truth

SEEING AS

Seeing and believing are not opposites, but two forms of *seeing-as*—that is, every form of understanding, even the most rational, rests on interpretive presuppositions.
To acknowledge this is of course impossible for dogmatic movements such as naturalism and Christian fundamentalism.
But what would it cost the individual researcher and the individual believer to acknowledge this shared ground?

TRUTH AS MOVEMENT

Classical epistemology seldom asked about the motive for knowledge. It silently assumed that there was one truth, and that all inquiry aimed to find it.
Adorno and others broke with this, seeing cognition as a perception that transforms the subject.
From that perspective, it hardly suffices to speak of one truth.
If not a striving toward shared truth, what then holds us together?

THE PRICE OF FALSEHOOD

Muriel Spark writes somewhere:

> *She did not know that the price of allowing false opinions was the gradual loss of one's capacity for forming true ones.*

But is it true?
Perhaps it is precisely by trying out and pretending false opinions that one learns to distinguish—and, at the right moment, insist—on the truth.

THE TRAP OF SELF-PRESENTATION

There is a point at which the communication of a new insight slides into self-presentation. It's as if the *homunculus* suddenly thinks: "Aha! What I'm saying now is new. I must behave like someone saying something new!"

Thus we shift from the fresh to the repeated. For self-presentation *is* presentation—a production of what is already known.

If the fresh is genuine (and that seems reasonable), is the repeated then false?

And in what does its falseness consist?

MY RESPONSIBILITY

Truth is in me, for me.

My responsibility is to pass it on when others might benefit from it . . .

On Perspectives

FROM MY SIDE

It strikes me that all the "reasonable" approaches come from the side of reason—that is, from a shared *nowhere.*

But surely I must approach from my side?

From where else?

Why should I approach anything from any perspective other than my own—not to mention from *no* perspective?

I must meet the "other" from my own position—and, if I wish, provisionally include others': my neighbor's, the prime minister's, or a supposedly neutral, rational "view from nowhere."

But always so that these other perspectives serve only as instruments for my own.

THE VIEW FROM NOWHERE

The *View from Nowhere* must, presumably, see everything from every possible position.

Including from within. When that is possible.

CHILD'S GAZE

The sad thing about parents not dying until one is an adult is that one no longer remembers how one saw them as a child. One has only memories.

And memory has not undergone the Kantian revolution.

CONTACT

Ontologies are representations—reductions of the real.

But when I ask, “What is *this*?” I do not want a representation; I want contact with it—to come closer to what is.

Is that too presumptuous a wish?

On Language

Small Words and Expressions

PROFESSIONAL LANGUAGE
"Yes, your mother perambulated yesterday."
The old woman had gone out into the street in her nightgown.
Precision is not always the professional language's greatest strength.

FEELING
Nietzsche notes (*Wille*, 479) that we only *have* a feeling once we've found a word for it.
The reverse, however, is not true: when someone says "I feel . . . ," there is only occasionally a feeling present.

WORDS
Nietzsche was right that our words for "inner states," such as will and thought, gather multiplicity under one label.
But that's what all words do.
And yet the right word can still redeem.

HAVE WE LOST SOMETHING?
A hundred years ago, "a weak will," "a sturdy character," and "a fine personality" were living expressions.
One could also say "his life" and "her fate"—not to mention "their souls."
All were countable nouns: a life, two lives, and so on.
What characterizes the words we use today?

Possibilities and Limitations

THE WORD'S CONDEMNATION

A man turned his "soft" face toward me.
I saw him but could not describe him properly.
My condemnation lay in the language itself: in my vocabulary, which gave me no words for what I saw from the neutral observer's position—that of objectivity, of love.

BEFORE LANGUAGE

Language (words) is not a precondition for perception.
It's obvious that people walk differently, though it's rarely possible to describe how they walk.
The articulation of visible difference seems to presuppose a theory or general view of bodily movement, such as those of bodywork instructors.
But the rest of us can still *see* something, even when we can't speak of it.

THE BRAIN'S REALITY

Valtteri Arstila writes:

> *When a professional bowler releases the ball, we experience its movement as smooth and continuous—without gaps, jolts, or blur. But experiments show that this picture is a construction: the seamless film we experience is the brain's own product.*

Thus the details we see but cannot describe exhaustively are not the details of reality, but of the brain's syntheses.
It is not "reality" that language fails to depict—but my own constructions.

BODY LANGUAGE I

On the bus I look out at the passing houses.

Thoughts and perceptions are tinged, positive or negative—and always accompanied by bodily sensation.

So bodily sensations are there when one notices them.

Judging by all the bodily metaphors—"uplifting," "heavy-hearted," "crushed"—they must once have been more vividly felt.

BODY LANGUAGE II

Lying in the dark, thinking of how tomorrow I'll impress my new acquaintance Arthur with my dissertation on Alfred Schütz, I notice my chest lifting, pushing out into the air—*puffing out his chest*. Another expression whose bodily grounding we've forgotten.

HUMILITY

Some mystics claim that the Ineffable is special because it cannot be adequately described. But the Ineffable is no more ineffable than countless other things: nothing we live among allows itself to be fully captured in language—even a withered leaf escapes exhaustive description. Perhaps the mystics should confine themselves to saying that the experience of the Ineffable differs from anything else they have ever experienced.

I DON'T KNOW WHAT TO CALL THIS NOTE:

I wrote in my notebook:

> *It's hard not to use God as a fix. When joy hits, prayer follows automatically. But now it also appears with each drop in mood—as a relief: I have God! Is it an abuse of prayer to regulate my mood with it? Do I use it to fix myself?*

As I wrote, I doubted my word choice. Was "drop" right? Should it be "mood level" or just "mood"?

Later, rereading the note, the doubt was gone: the written had become the thought itself. Whatever may have been there before was gone.

THE POEM AND THE NOTE

There is an uncertainty in note-writing that does not exist in poetry. A poem must either be abandoned or felt: *That's how it should be!*

Most notes feel: *Was that really what I meant?*

THE GATE OF LANGUAGE

It is only through language's holding fast to states like anger or sorrow that distinctions and borderlands between them emerge.

Without language there are no discrete states or transitions—only the river's flow, only This.

And without language, we could not even ask whether there exist "negative states" with properties opposite to the one we are studying.

Here language opens the gate to the unknown.

YES! THAT'S HOW IT IS!

And then there are insights that fall straight out of language itself, letting the whole body yield in grateful relief:
Yes! That's how it is!

LANGUAGE AND INQUIRY

While writing, one often discovers that one does not know what one thought one knew.
Definitions crumble, implications appear, connections emerge—some real, others imagined.
Writing is therefore not mere reproduction but inquiry.
Language reduces—and enriches.

AFTER BEAUTY I

To say *That's beautiful!* is to step away.
Before, there was only This: I and it, one.
In the word we separate, and our being-together is washed away in the stream of words.

AFTER BEAUTY II

To say *That's beautiful!* is to step closer.
Before, there were only the other and me, two.
In the word we join, and in the being-together we flow away as one.

THE SMILE

The one who smiles at another sees the other *in* the smile.
And he has no words for what he sees.
So Jaspers (among others) was wrong to claim that we meet the other in language.
The meeting in language can never be more than an approximation.

The Language in the Detail

THE CAUSE OF THE MOMENT

An answer to "Why?" is never quite genuine.
The motive is unique to the person and the act, while language can only mirror our shared stock of acceptable reasons:

> –*Why did you leave me?*
>
> –*Because the moon was green that day.*

No? And yet language demands a "Why?" precisely for the acts that matter most.
You'd think it got paid to confuse us.

WHEN LANGUAGE FALLS SILENT

What does God tell us through our inability to describe the world—or even a leaf?
And what does he add in the instant when a poem or a word appears both necessary and sufficient—where nothing can be added, nothing taken away?

THE BARRIER

Texts have borders.
There are paths in them that lead down to a barrier—and those are the ones you shouldn't take?

HEAVY WORDS

Why is it only when we face the great losses in another person's life that we ask ourselves: *What should I say?*
And why does reflection awaken only then?
Why do we feel language's heaviness exactly where we most need its unimpeded flow?
Perhaps it's wisest to stick to the fact:
At great losses, words grow heavy.
And let them stay heavy.

Lessons from the Wayside

The Conditions

WE LIVE WHERE WE LIVE

In projects, in ownerships, in original sin, in guilt, in the body, and in the limitations of language: we live where we live.
And we live in history.
Thus today it makes no sense to fight rationalization—or its particular manifestations, such as the future use of big data to impose psychoeducational treatment programs upon us. These developments set the frame for the life we can lead.
The space of freedom lies within the matrix.

THE GREY PACKAGE

The optimal life circumstances for the spiritual journey are said to be those that are hardest for us to bear:
illness and suffering, stigma and exclusion, war and political persecution, poverty, loss of status, and the loss of those we love.
The gift I received was addiction—the one that let me see all my ambitions, and everything that had made my life worth living at the time, collapse around me.
But perhaps the true gift was that I was allowed to unwrap it?

The Method

You are only as sick as your secrets.
—Wisdom from AA

TAKING STOCK

Just as the prudent captain inspects his ship before setting the day's course, so should the prudent man take stock of himself before taking stock of the day's possibilities and challenges.

It all begins within. Before the galley is cleaned, there is no room for fresh fish.

Why am I afraid of him?

Why am I angry?

Repeated fear and repeated anger always point back at me:

What did I do—if only in thought—against him?

What did I fail to do?

THE PRICE OF INNOCENCE

The pure in heart can never come to know themselves.

For they never have the occasion to ask,

Why on earth did I do that?

THE SADDEST SECRET

For several years I would say, every six months, that I had once again been freed from a sad secret I hadn't known I carried.

Yet in each of us there is a sadder secret that drives us through the world. And I cannot imagine what would happen if I opened myself to it.

". . . and more will be revealed"

SELF-OVERCOMING
Self-overcoming moves in circles.
At first, I boiled with anger at young people who put their feet up on the train seats.
Then I began to say, *Get your feet down!*
Later it became, *Would you be so kind as to put your feet on the floor? Thank you so much!*
Today I say nothing again.
What might the next step be?
Polishing their shoes?

NIETZSCHE WAS WRONG
One should not live every day as if it were one's last.
Rather, one should live every day as if one knew that a million tomorrows would follow this day.

WHAT IS
Just like action, the eye seeks what is perfect and rejects the imperfect.
The trick is to see the perfection of the imperfect in its own form.

GRACE AND WILL
The good person has no defenses, says Knausgård of Prince Myshkin.
Goodness cannot be willed—one can only hope, that grace will let it descend into one.
Without hoping for it.

ON COMING HOME

To become oneself, to come home to oneself—
it's not like a seatbelt, where you hear the tongue click into the lock.
When you come home to yourself, you suddenly discover that you've been home for a while. *When* the bolt slid into place, you don't know. You only know that you are home.
The same goes for falling out of oneself.
At first it feels like an objectless sorrow. Later you realize:
It's myself that I have lost!
But *when* it happened, you never find out.
Unlike when you lift the latch and draw the bolt from the lock.

THE NECESSARY DETOUR

The convert has made himself into an object.
But conversions are necessary steps
on the way home.

MY TEACHER IS CAUGHT IN THE SWAMP

My teacher is caught in the swamp.
From the swamp he illumines the path for me.
The swamp illumines the path for me.

PEANUT BUTTER AND JELLY

Others have walked this path before me—greater souls, better suited to take in all its beauty.
And yet they too were only peanut butter and jelly.

Last

Forgiveness *is* here.
And yet my fingers tremble, and my soul quivers.

When Leaving the Palace

Forty-odd Glimpses from a Traveling Prince

Setting Out

The Balloon

I am a balloon
A little red balloon
In a stormy sky

Clouds chase me
Winds tear at me
Lightning hunts for me

I am a little red balloon
But I am safe
Your fickle fingers hold the string.

Wail My Longing

Oh, YES! sweet ache
shine forth from the heart

shine on the trees
and make them shudder

shine on the houses
and make them tremble

shine on the cars
and make them wail
my longing into the sky.

Take Me on Your Breath

O sweet Mother, sweetest Mother
take me on your breath!
Blow me high into the storm
let the thunder shake me
Blow me through the darkest jungle
let the tigers claw me
Blow me deep into the earth
let the iron burn me.

O sweet Mother, sweetest mother
take me on your breath
Blow me into poverty
let my need efface me
Blow me into infamy
let my shame dissolve me
Blow me into loneliness
and leave me there forever.

O sweet Mother, sweetest Mother
take me on you breath
Blow me far, and farther still
Blow me through the ages
Blow me where no name nor form
joins me to this moment.
O sweet Mother, sweetest Mother
take me on your breath.

Please, Mother!

Scratch the crust in my heart
My longing is itching

Wrench open the muscle
The fibres are yearning

Stab me, please, Mother!
Start my sweet blood flowing!

I Draw the World

Up through my foot
and into the room
Into this chaos of chairs and tables
where straight lines despair of running their courses
Into these pillows
laden with attraction
And into this air
barraged by photons and other constructions
Up through my foot and into all this
I draw the world.

The Gate to Love

Don't dress my wound
Sweet sister Honey
For misery is the gate to love.

Don't dress my wound
But let anger inflame it
Indolence sleep in it and
Vanity sprout from it.
For misery is the gate to love.

And don't ease my pain
Sweet sister Honey.
For misery is the gate to love.

Don't ease my pain
Let it gloss my envy
Energize my fear and
Empower my greed.
For misery is the gate to love.

But please stay near me
My sweet sister Honey
So that misery may be
The gate to love.

Factories of My Mind

There! Do you see the Black Prince
and his sweet sister, Honey
prospecting for tenderness
in the factories of my mind?

I have mined those old dumps myself
excavating whatever resentments, fears and miscellaneous miseries
I could find. And the ore was good and plenty!
But now that Black Prince prospects there.

Looking in on the Relatives

The Seeker

I walk the earth
Heavily, slowly I walk the earth
When will I arrive?

I walk time
Heavily, slowly I walk time
When will I arrive?

I walk me
Heavily, slowly I walk me
When will I arrive?

The Daughter

Woman, immobile,
at her sink
Locked in a prison
behind her glasses
Mama calling
her to come out.

The Innocent

A lovely sweet-spewing sentimentalist am I.
Bureaucrats melt between my fingers
Jacobs and Jacobins thaw in my heart
(weary bus drivers too).
For I am the admirer of unfashionable girls,
the lover of disputants, and of unwashed bodies.

Innocence is my vocation
smiles and laughter my produce
tears and sighs the tools of my trade.
Little children look at me
acknowledging knowings shared.
A lovely sweet-spewing sentimentalist am I!

The Jester

I am an ingenious soul who
delights in teasing the humans.

So once I put on a cleft palate
and the difficultest language invented

Spending that lifetime on giving long talks
on the urgent impracticality

Of human understanding.

A Poet on the Range

Upright in his saddle
he scans the horizon for true adventure
and spurns the modest verse

With lovely young faces, so innocent
they seep into boots and up his jeans
knowing he's Mr. Right

But always finding something lacking
(a fleck on the nightie, an unpolished nail
a reason not sufficient for joy)

himself lacking love, or begrudging them babies
(which I don't know) he commands his dog
to chase them away.

Uncle Evergreen

Yes, I am far into the fifties
but I can revert to 43
I can revert to hopeful trembling
and terrified timid kindness.
But I never was a botanist.

I was a battered wife, you know
a young Muslim girl
a yellow tooth and
a nostril surprised.
But never a botanist, no.

I am a strutting berry
eager to throw my seeds.
I am a pea pod, an acorn and . . .
What is this swelling?
. . . a budding eyeglass lanyard???

En Route to Voltaire

Man's Mission

Man's mission is
to provide all matter
with a soul.

This is why the primitives
speak to their Gods
in the antelope, the rock, and the sea:

To prepare them for the day
when man's mission
has been accomplished.

I Am an Illusion

The self is a hideout conceived by the soul
built by the ego and run by capital.

Capital was written by Marx (and by Engels)
and the ego by Freud all alone.

But the soul was written by God knows who
and so I am just an illusion.

Unity

Bodhis are busying
Soaking up karma
Of cryhearts watching
Trickling salt water
Breaking down bodhis.

Stars in Their Spaces

A Smile Is Sitting Gently

Inviting the guests to slam the door
requesting the puke to soil the floor
inciting the noise to play some more
enjoying the Crash!
savouring the Boom!
a smile is sitting
gently

A Prince on the Bus

I have God's pimples on my heart
and his bedsores on my brain.
In the bus I must hide my lovely eyes
to prevent a popular eruption.

Let's Start

The morning-contented belly heaves:
We're full, let's start.

He runs for the bus,
runs for his life.
Having fun.

He looks at the calendar.
There's a whole month after this one.
A whole month! What a marvel!

He looks into a corner,
and there you are, playing with the dust.
Then you move on, taking your helpmate with you.

He puts muck on his fingers
Smells it, waits, and smells again:
It's gone.

He listens to the heartbeat.
Which is more beautiful: The black plastic bag
Or the orange tulip? He cannot tell.

He rubs her feet.
Birds sing sweetly on the river of repose.
He thinks travel agenting is a great career.

He closes his eyes, and . .
The morning-contented belly heaves:
We're full, let's start.

We Ride a Cosy Cosmos

A mile from here the moon is slowly spinning,
while far-off Mars is calmly standing still.
Close by we see the sunlit earth revolving
and hear the ether whistle in her trees.
Yes, certainly, we ride a cosy cosmos!

In the Summer, in the City

Neutral the Prince rolls through the city
sucking up heat, blowing comfort,
grudging no one his praise.
One with the sun,
one with its suffering children.

Luminous Night

A plastic moon is shining through the window
A little rodent gnaws at the attention
and I am farting
peaceably.

Travellers—and Their Companions

The Lion and His Keeper

A silly lion skips through the house
On the walls, fondly
A laughing bird follows.

The Heart and the Hawthorn

The blossoming hawthorn deflowers the heart.
Willingly he opens to her
and steals her virginity.

The Cat and the Peacock

Sinking through the water the cat blows bubbles round the peacock.
Avidly he pecks at them,
has yet to learn the water's play.

The Wave and the Sea

The little wave sighs daintily
Saying it's afraid of the fish in the deep.
And the sea smiles patiently.

Meeting the Old Woman and the Heartbeat

Did I Die, or What?

(Six Stories about the Heartbeat)

The ovum is pushed from side to side,
the womb is stretched to the limit.
When the beating ceases
the infant showers itself with stars.

The lovely mother bobs down the street
In longing his eyes follow her movement.
The attention flags, wanes,
then goes elsewhere.

The ball pops over the net
not certain of its right to the serve.
Slower and slower the oatmeal is stirred.
Mama is tired.

Eagerly the tongue beats on the bell.
The sun dyes the pane a fluorescent red.
The nuggets swirl, round and round.
After the shower the bell is refreshed.

The beating grows slower, the hammer melts,
and molten metal swirls into unmoving air.
When the shower has subsided the giant codfish opens its mouth
rhythmically revealing nightskies of stars.

The heartbeat slows down, then becomes indistinct.
Before it stops a new pulse starts up.
So he never finds out
did I die, or what?

I Hunger for the Old Woman

I sit on the seesaw, one of many.
Rice pours through my body.
But I hunger for an old woman.

The lovely mother offers her breast
and the sweet sister touches my thigh.
But I hunger for the old woman.

My body is swollen
and my heart trembles.
But I hunger only for the old woman.

I touch my breast, I touch my thigh.
And it is sweet.
But still I hunger for the old woman.

Slow Waves Breaking on Dissolving Rocks

Slow waves break upon dissolving rocks
leading to slow waves breaking on dissolving rocks.
Finally the coast is empty.

A duckling bounces down the trail from its hiding place
                                                            behind the boulders.
Entering the water the duck becomes a canoe
                                                            firmly paddled out to sea.
In mid-stroke the paddle interrupts its circle, going off somewhere . . .

The old woman pops her head over the rim.
The waters flee towards the coasts
wave after wave destroying itself against the sides of the bowl.

The old woman ducks out of sight. Gradually
slow wave after slow wave again breaks upon dissolving rocks
leading to slow waves breaking on dissolving rocks.

He Returns to the Heartbeat

Aflame with the old woman he sits in the driveway
kissing the tires as her car cruises by.
But her cats spit at him
and he returns to the heartbeat.

Delightful Detours

1

I spread your breasts all over my body
and soak them into my bones.
Kindly your eyes drink in my longing
pouring it back into mine.

2

A longing breaks lose from incautious eye-balls
Revels in his freedom amidst specs and mascara
Ends up in a fight against pummelling lashes
Returning back home
A sadder, not wiser yearning.

3

(Kore)

You come to me soaked in adoration
In the milk that flows from my nipples
In the tears that I rain.

You straddle me then flick me aside
When the sparrow chirrups
Or a nettle caresses your thigh.

You pass me through the frankness of your eye
Hang my medals in your closet and
Remain unseduced.

We pray for little fears and follies. But not you
Untouched by my thunder, unfettered
You forge on.

4

Is this the Heartache Road? She asks
and prepares to get up from her seat.
It is, he says, but it's a very long road.
Is this then, she asks, where it begins?
Oh yes, he sighs. This is where it begins.

On the Fate of Sailors

On the Fate of Sailors

I am but a victim of this woman
says the captain of the ship as
he musters his crew of magnificent sons.

We mate, have children and search for God
without knowing why. In each of us a life is sunk
while spray caresses her breasts.

I am her child by the youngest son
You see me with him, the last in line
of the sailors on the Enterprise.

Who suck, each night, on marvellous tits
while on deck walks the captain idly feeding
children to the dolphins.

I too will go overboard one night
to romp on waves and under keels
all over Amphitrite's realm.

Only to be drunk by a captain's son
as he sucks the spray and spews his sperm
through the hull of the Enterprise.

In Strange Lands and Beautiful Times

A Scenario

I hear heavy walking up in the clouds
Footsteps that crunch on the sand in my ear
Someone is there. And you may pray, bird, pray.

Inside the bowl the big wave is churning
Churning, so impatient for the roar of the sea
I hear heavy walking up in the clouds.

Up on land boulder falls over boulder
Small stones are shot, shot deep into the earth
Someone is there. And you may pray, bird, pray.

The windshield wiper grinds to a halt and
The little kangaroo hops the last pages
I hear heavy walking up in the clouds.

Perhaps the bowl broke, perhaps the book closed
Certainly order has slipped away. Yet
Someone is there. And you may pray, bird, pray.

Dancing the ocean, catching fish that jump
He can't be bothered by boulders or books
I hear heavy walking up in the clouds
Someone is there. And you may pray, bird, pray.

In Arcadia

Few steps from death, and not yet screaming
In unmolten skies full of sweet snow for melting
Pale boys smile finely, inanely at nothing

Exquisitely hurting or bored to the bone
Dancers are mating while order runs wild
Few steps from death, and not yet screaming

Back from the ball-room the dancers hoist rafters
Steeling the sky against sweet melting snowflakes
Pale boys smile finely, inanely at nothing

Mothers in time lose their large open faces
Inspecting steel rafters for rust and corrosion
Few steps from death, and not yet screaming

Fathers are pining away on their sofas
Say they need nothing yet feel incomplete
Pale boys smile finely, inanely at nothing

We all want the perfect to ape imperfection
Tits without bras and cocks that don't bite. Yet
Pale boys smile finely, inanely at nothing
Few steps from death, and still not screaming.

There's a Need for Longing

Sitting at home in white wedding dresses
lovely young mothers are looking for jobs.
There's a need for longing, so much longing.

Whirling through spaces handsome young cadets
pierce stunted secrets. Meanwhile their brides wait
sitting at home in white wedding dresses.

Ads show you pictures of loving grannies
and of sweet adolescents. All true, but
there's a need for longing, so much longing.

Where do you come from, beautiful pictures?
Where do you lead space cadets and mothers
sitting at home in white wedding dresses?

Dread rises up, it's not good enough! The
grease spots won't yield, the space ship is crashing.
There's a need for longing, so much longing.

When the world walks out of The Bridal Suite
the heart opens up. That's what it takes, not
sitting at home in white wedding dresses.
There's a need for longing, much more longing.

August (2004)

Idiot boy throws emeralds in the air
Old man sweeps pebbles off the pavement
While soft slanting light whispers ”autumn”

Black luminous beetle, felled, on his back
Bares shimmering turquoises soon forgotten
Idiot boy throws emeralds in the air

Old man and idiot boy admire
Young breasts scenting the sweet summer breeze
While soft slanting light whispers ”autumn”

Eyes seek brilliance, a wasp shits in air
Mutely dragon flies stand over Baghdad
Idiot boy throws emeralds in the air

Kissed on the lips by the last dying wasp
Old man pulls back, and satori slinks off
While soft slanting light whispers ”autumn”

We sit all day long with the dying wasp
Old man ponders the pebbles he's lost
Idiot boy throws emeralds in the air
And the soft slanting light whispers ”autumn”.

September

Idiot boy sits by the wayside
Adoring young girls in their Friday tits
Enjoying his hunger.

Out on the tarmac frog has stopped leaping
There for a moment desire is not streaming
God has plugged up the tubes.

Back in the yard chain saw is roaring
Protesting that while Summer is tit-time
Autumn and Spring belong to the thighs

Idiot boy sits listening to chain saw
Hears the sigh between anger and raging
Salutes the desperate struggle

(Between the towers of thunder and lightning
Inside the sigh, God's voice is resting.
Its echoes are flying all over the place.

(Sometimes it's nice just to let yourself wander
Adrift in the fertile confusion of mind
Flying on echoes.))

Tick is caught without chance in a paint blob
Freed he burrows into the finger. Tweaked off
The pact is not broken.

Dying grasshopper flies out to greet him
Hitting idiot boy like a thirst. Rests on his breath
What a fine place to go!

Winds are thinning and few dogs are whelping
God is preparing his holiday cruise
Idiot boy is laughing.

In Bix Box Land

A Christmas Carol

A thing of Thee
is a heron is a heron
A thing of Thee
there are no calm causes

Driven I sing of Thee
of Thy calm causes and reasons
A thing of Thee
there are no mistakes
A thing of Thee
is a heron is a heron
A thing of Thee I think
there will be no mistakes
A thing of Thee
the heron circles the forbidden city
And his trumpet sounds
And he's watched from the tower
by angel eyes

So I thing of Thee
is a heron is a heron.

Hymn

In Bix Box Land little blind raisins
fly—undiluted—with wives and longings
while angel eyes look on.

No voices there call out for lawyers.
Nor do Boxers engage night nurses
to watch over handsome dreams.

Yet pacing needs the pain of lawyers
as hallways and landways need their pacing.
And handsome dreams need watching.

So I myself will call them out:
True me, Bix Box, true me, please!
True me into clear nexality
True me into cherry spots, fly and flew!

Rack me truly, Bix Box, please!
Rack me from the wet stigmata
Rack me into cherry spots, fly and flew!

Hoe me through the boxes, Bix Box Thing!
Hoe me into tired muscle, true to stagnant blood
Hoe me into cherry spots, fly and flew!

True me wholly, Hallow Tole!
Rack me Rimnal, holesome Hale!
Rackal ruesome Ho!

Thus fly me, raisin, fly me home
through handsome dreams and lawyers' pains
to angel eyes, to wife and longing, fly me home!

www.ingramcontent.com/pod-product-compliance
Lightning Source LLC
LaVergne TN
LVHW050636100826
845148LV00011B/1885

* 9 7 9 8 3 8 5 2 7 3 4 2 3 *